First Reconciliation

Dr. Gerard F. Baumbach
Moya Gullage

Rev. Msgr. John F. Barry
Dr. Eleanor Ann Brownell
Helen Hemmer, I.H.M.
Gloria Hutchinson
Dr. Norman F. Josaitis
Rev. Michael J. Lanning, O.F.M.
Dr. Marie Murphy
Dr. Mary O'Grady
Karen Ryan
Joseph F. Sweeney

Official Theological Consultant
Most Rev. Edward K. Braxton, Ph. D., S.T.D.

Pastoral Consultant
Rev. Virgilio P. Elizondo, Ph. D., S.T.D.

Catechetical and Liturgical Consultants
Dr. Gerard F. Baumbach
Dr. Eleanor Ann Brownell

William H. Sadlier, Inc.
9 Pine Street
New York, NY 10005–1002

Nihil Obstat

✠ Most Reverend George O. Wirz

Censor Librorum

Imprimatur

✠ Most Reverend William H. Bullock

Bishop of Madison

October 20, 1995

The *Nihil Obstat* and *Imprimatur* are official declarations
that a book or pamphlet is free of doctrinal or moral error.
No implication is contained therein that those who have
granted the *Nihil Obstat* and *Imprimatur* agree with the
contents, opinions, or statements expressed.

Home Office:
9 Pine Street
New York, NY 10005–1002

ISBN: 0-8215-2411-9
23456789/987

Acknowledgments

Excerpts and adaptations from *Good News Bible*,
copyright © American Bible Society 1966, 1971, 1976, 1979.

Excerpts from the *New American Bible*, copyright © 1991,
1986, 1970 by the Confraternity of Christian Doctrine (CCD),
Washington, D.C. Used with permission.

This *First Reconciliation Guide* was guided and inspired by the
Catechism of the Catholic Church. Points of reference for each
chapter of the guide are indicated throughout.

Contents

A Complete Sacramental Preparation

Purpose

The purpose of Sadlier's *First Reconciliation* is rooted in giving children a beginning experience of what it means to know right from wrong, to be sorry, and to make up or reconcile. It helps them understand, in a manner consonant with their psychological development, everyone's need both to ask forgiveness and to give forgiveness. The aim is that early positive experience of this sacrament as one of peace and forgiveness will also motivate them to celebrate the sacrament on a regular basis after their First Reconciliation.

Sadlier's *First Reconciliation* is designed to help catechists engage the First Reconciliation children, their families, and the whole parish so that:

❖ sacrament preparation truly becomes a significant moment for ongoing faith formation in the lives, not only of the children, but also of the family and the parish.

❖ the children are prepared within a formative faith community to celebrate with reverence, understanding, and hope the sacrament of Reconciliation for the first time.

❖ the catechesis of Reconciliation presented is accurate, complete, and consistent with Vatican II theology and liturgy and the *Catechism of the Catholic Church*.

Sadlier's *First Reconciliation* does this in six sessions, each containing:

❖ **a Scripture story** that provides a framework for understanding the aspect of Reconciliation being explained

❖ a "child-level" **catechesis** of the part of the sacrament of Reconciliation being presented

❖ a special page set apart to help the children see, in summary fashion, key ideas of the session, including: *How to Make a Loving Choice*; *Living the Ten Commandments*; *An Act of Contrition*; *An Examination of Conscience*; *Steps to Celebrate the Sacrament*; and, *How to Bring Peace to Others*

❖ creative **activities** and **questions** in every lesson to engage the child's imagination, memory, and reasoning powers

❖ a **Family Focus** section and an **At Home** activity encouraging and assisting parental involvement in the preparation process

Options for Sacramental Preparation

Sadlier's sacramental program provides easy-to-use materials that offer a variety of options for parish use:

❖ the traditional parish preparation for First Reconciliation, directed by the catechist, actively involving the family

❖ parents preparing their own children for the sacrament with the support of the catechist and the parish staff

❖ parish-organized family groups, which the catechist guides and directs, empowered to take primary responsibility for the First Reconciliation preparation of their children

In each of these options, the children with their families celebrate First Reconciliation with the prayer and support of the whole parish community.

First Reconciliation: Scope and Sequence

	Chapter Theme	Scripture	Reconciliation	Family Focus
1	**Following Jesus** CCC: 386, 1779	The Forgiving Father (Luke 15:11–24)	Jesus shows us how to make loving choices	Preparing for choices
2	**Following God's Law** CCC: 1962, 1968	The Greatest Commandment (Matthew 22:35–39)	Living the Ten Commandments; sin	Understanding God's law
3	**Being Sorry, Being Forgiven** CCC: 1430–33	The Forgiven Woman (Luke 7:36–40, 44–50)	The meaning of sorrow and forgiveness; an Act of Contrition	Saying "I'm sorry" at home
4	**Examination of Conscience** CCC: 1454, 1779	The Lost Sheep (Luke 15:4–7)	Examination of conscience	Formation of conscience
5	**Celebrating Reconciliation** CCC: 1443, 1456, 1458	Zacchaeus (Luke 19:1–10)	Celebrating the sacrament	Preparing to celebrate Reconciliation
6	**Living as Peacemakers** CCC: 1829, 1832	Jesus and the Children (Mark 10:13–16)	Sharing the peace of Christ	The family as peacemakers

CCC = *Catechism of the Catholic Church*

A Family and Parish-Based Preparation

The Role of the Catechist

The catechist in this program has the delightful task of actively involving and working with the family to prepare the child to celebrate First Reconciliation. The catechist needs to be prepared, enthusiastic, loving, and, above all, reverent before the uniqueness and dignity of each child.

The catechist, therefore, needs to know each child under his/her care. A genuine effort should be made to be in touch with the families of all the children in the program, encouraging their participation, especially through the *Family Focus* section and in the opening and closing rites.

The Role of the Director

The preparation of children for First Reconciliation is essential to the ongoing life of the parish. The director's role is at the heart of the network that involves the children, their families, the catechist, the pastor, and the parish. Ways in which the director can provide leadership in sacramental preparation include:

❖ planning and directing meetings with families involved in sacramental preparation;

❖ discerning ways to help parents reflect on the meaning of Reconciliation in their own lives;

❖ informing and involving the parish community in the sacramental preparation, rites, and celebration of First Reconciliation.

The Role of the Parish Community

The sacrament of Reconciliation is a sacrament of communal peace through which sins committed after Baptism are forgiven. As such it is imperative that the parish be involved as much as possible in the preparation of its children and their families for the celebration of First Reconciliation. If both are to be nourished in a formative faith community, the participation of the parish, especially through a communal celebration of Reconciliation, is very important.

Sadlier's *First Reconciliation* preparation facilitates this with the opening and closing rites—both of which are intended to be celebrated with the community.

The parish community should not only participate in these rites by their prayers and presence, but do all it can to support and encourage the young believers.

The Role of the Family

While some families might choose to prepare their own children for the sacrament of Reconciliation, it is important that *all* families see that it is not necessarily (or entirely) in formal catechetical sessions that children develop an understanding of the sacrament. Children come to understand God's constant and persistent love as they see it modeled in that of their families. They learn what it means to reconcile when reconciliation is celebrated in the home and they learn forgiveness by being forgiven.

To help in these important tasks, a take-home section, *Suggestions for Family*, is provided on pages 23–24. Duplication of these pages is permitted and encouraged.

Where the program is catechist-directed, we suggest that the children bring their books home to share with their families. In each session there is a *Family Focus* section and an *At Home* activity to encourage parental involvement. Parents and families are also asked to participate in the opening and closing prayer celebrations.

Family Focus

This lesson on examination of conscience is a very important one for young children. It should be presented in the context of the love and care God has for them especially as expressed, at least in part, in the love and care they experience at home and in the faith community. We do not want our children to become guilt-ridden or scrupulous. Yet we must help them become aware of their responsibilities as baptized members of the Church. We also want to help them to become aware of the great love and mercy of Christ, who supports them when they do what is right and who forgives them when they do what is wrong.

Conscience is that awareness we have about the rightness or wrongness of our choices. In young children it should be developed gently and consistently.

1. Read through the lesson together. Invite your child to tell you the story of the lost sheep. Ask how we are like the lost sheep when we do what is wrong.

2. Go over the questions for an examination of conscience on page 35. Your child might want to suggest other or different questions. You might want to add ones that you find helpful.

3. Pray together the words of the song your child learned on page 36. Then help your child do the **At Home** activity.

At Home

Help the shepherd find the lost sheep. Use a crayon or marker.

After you help the shepherd find the lost sheep, pray this prayer with your family.

† Jesus, You are our Good Shepherd. You guide and protect us. Help us always to make loving choices. Amen.

37

Components

Child's Book: First Reconciliation

The child's book presents 6 eight-page sessions, including a *Family Focus* and *At Home* activity page for each session to encourage and assist parental involvement in the preparation process.

It also includes two rites to be celebrated with the community: *A Preparation Rite* at the beginning of the preparation and *A Peacemaking Rite* at its end.

The book also includes:

❖ *Summary: I Will Remember*—a review of key ideas

❖ *Preparing for Reconciliation Booklets*—one for each session—for the child to share at home

❖ the *Rites of Reconciliation*—easy reference to the steps involved in the individual and communal rites

❖ additional prayers and songs

❖ a *Peacemaker Checklist*—ideas for bringing peace to others

❖ *Prayer Partners Invitation*—suggestions for involving parishioners and children as prayer partners

❖ certificate of First Reconciliation

❖ activity cutouts to accompany two sessions and the *Preparation Rite*

Catechist's/Leader's Guide

This guide provides a clear 24-page presentation of the material in the child's book. A scope and sequence for the program is included and easy-to-use suggestions are made for each session in a simple "beginning, middle, end" format.

A Children's Mass Book: With Jesus Always

This little keepsake book is available in two editions, soft cover and deluxe hard cover. It is intended to serve, not only as a beautiful memento of the child's celebration of First Reconciliation and First Eucharist, but as an ongoing source of prayer.

Besides the prayers of the Mass, it contains a section on how to prepare for and celebrate the sacrament of Reconciliation. Traditional prayers and practices of the Catholic Church are also included.

First Reconciliation Music

The cassette or compact disk, *Songs: First Reconciliation*, contains all the songs and hymns in the child's book. Each song is arranged for and sung by children in a simple and inviting way.

A First Reconciliation Certificate

Besides the certificate contained in the child's book, a separate deluxe edition, suitable for framing, is available.

A First Reconciliation Heart Memento

A sturdy golden-roped heart embossed with the words "Jesus, I give You my heart" is available for the children to wear as they celebrate Reconciliation and to keep as a memento.

A Preparation Rite

Purpose

From the very beginning the preparation process for First Reconciliation should be rooted in realization that the celebration of the sacrament is an *ecclesial* event, a celebration of the Church. Just as sin has a harmful effect on the whole community, reconciliation heals not only the sinner but the whole people of God.

For this reason the children preparing to receive Reconciliation come before their parish community at Sunday Mass to ask for prayers and support.

Scheduling the Rite

It is suggested that this *Preparation Rite* be celebrated at a regularly scheduled Sunday liturgy (or Saturday evening) after the first session of preparation. This allows for the children to receive their books and to have the rite explained to them ahead of time. Parents or guardians can be apprised of their part in the rite through a personal invitation from the catechist.

It will be important also to speak to the pastor and the celebrant to decide at which point in the Mass the rite will take place. An appropriate time would be immediately before the final blessing of the Mass. Copies of the rite should be given in advance to the pastor and the celebrant.

Adapt the rite to the number of children involved and to the constraints and possibilities of your parish church. For example, you might choose to seat parents directly behind their child so that the parental blessing may be easily done.

Involvement of the Parish Community

It is appropriate that the presiding priest or the catechist give the assembly a *brief* introduction to the rite—an explanation of the children's desire to receive the sacrament, the parents' blessing of their children, and the community's recognition of its responsibility to support and pray for these young members of the Church.

Parent/Guardian Involvement

We suggest that parents or guardians be sent a letter requesting their participation in the preparation rite. A follow-up reminder call would be helpful as well. You might want to send them a copy of the rite and encourage them to bring it to Mass with them. Remind the families to have the children bring their books to Mass also. Just in case (young children can be notoriously forgetful), have extra copies of the rite on hand at Mass.

Ask the families to come a little early for Mass so that you can arrange seating and go over the rite together.

Preparation with the Children

❖ Read through the rite together, explaining what will take place. Help the children become more aware that they belong to a parish community that wants to support and pray for them.

❖ Help the children cut out the "Jesus the Good Shepherd" figure in the back of their books. Explain how it will be used during the rite. You might want to collect and save all the cutouts until the Mass.

❖ Have the children listen to the song on the cassette or CD and sing along until they are comfortable with it.

❖ Encourage them to bring their books home and go over the rite with the family member(s) who will be with them at Mass.

❖ Have each child write in his or her book the time at which Mass will be celebrated.

1 Following Jesus

Adult Background

In the biblical story of Hosea, God must choose between destroying or embracing the faithless people of Israel. As God considers allowing this faithless nation to be delivered into its enemies' hands, He says: "My heart will not let me do it! My love for you is too strong" (Hosea 11:8).

Likewise in the story of the forgiving father, the father can either reject his wayward son or welcome him home. Love dictates forgiveness. And the son's choice to throw himself on his father's mercy is vindicated. Because the elder son chooses to be angry and self-righteous, he refuses to join the feast.

We are formed by the choices we make for or against love. Despite our good intentions, we experience the inner conflict Saint Paul described: "I don't do what I would like to do, but instead I do what I hate" (Romans 7:15). When we violate the Law of Love, there is always a way to come home again. The sacrament of Reconciliation offers us an opportunity like that given to the lost son.

Through the ministry of the Church, we are forgiven and restored to full relationship with God and the faith community. The seeds of our loving choices are once again watered by mercy.

Preparation Hints

Prepare in advance the place where your group will meet. Make the environment as pleasing, welcoming, and prayerful as possible. Some ways to do this include: preparing a prayer corner with an open Bible, having soft music playing as the children enter, displaying flowers and posters, arranging chairs in a circle in one part of the room and desks or working surfaces in another. Sometimes it helps to have a special sound, such as a chime, to signal a time of prayer.

Special-Needs Child

Provide an atmosphere of acceptance in which all the children can realize how special they are.

Visual Needs
❖ large print chart of steps in making choices

Auditory Needs
❖ headphones, tape recording of the Scripture story

Tactile-Motor Needs
❖ partners to assist in the "What Is a Choice?" activity, and *Preparing for Reconciliation* booklet 1

Resources

We Celebrate God's Peace (video) *Children of Praise* series, vol. 2
Treehaus Communications, Inc.
P.O. Box 249
Loveland, OH 45140–0249
(1–800–638–4287)

Materials for This Session

❖ Sadlier's *Songs*: *First Reconciliation* cassette

Plan for the Session

Beginning ___ min.

❖ Greet the children warmly, calling each one by name. Give each child a copy of *First Reconciliation*. Read the title together and invite comments about the front cover.

Have the children open their books to page 6. Talk about the many ways in which the children are growing—especially in their knowledge and love of God. Read the first two paragraphs and invite the children to share their responses. Then invite them to make the sign of the cross slowly and reverently.

Read the first three paragraphs on page 7 and invite the children to share their ideas. Ask them to explain what choices the children in the pictures are thinking about. Then introduce the Bible story by reading the last paragraph.

Middle ___ min.

❖ Point out the image of the candle and Bible on page 8. Tell the children that this image marks the Scripture story page. Have the children gather to listen to a wonderful story that Jesus told. Have the children look at the illustration on page 9. Ask them to identify the part of the story that is illustrated. Then discuss the children's reactions to the story by asking the questions at the bottom of the page. Emphasize that Jesus told the story so that people would understand the greatness of God's forgiving love for us.

❖ Talk together with the children about making choices. Explain that we can make good choices or bad choices. Then tell the children that Jesus showed us how to make good choices. Read aloud the first three paragraphs on page 10.

Display the words *choice, mistake,* and *accident*. Help the children to understand the difference between a free choice and an accident or mistake.

Some examples of accidents: spilling milk on the floor; breaking a window while playing ball. Help the children to see that such things are *accidents*. They were not chosen on purpose.

Some examples of mistakes: picking up someone's box of crayons thinking they were yours; not doing homework because the book was left at school. Help the children see that such things are *mistakes*. They were not done on purpose.

❖ Review the concepts of mistakes and accidents by reading the fourth paragraph. Ask the questions at the end of the page. Go over the steps for making good choices on page 11.

Ask the children to identify the choice being made in each picture.

End ___ min.

❖ Help the children recall the difference between a deliberate wrong choice and a mistake or an accident by reading over the case studies on page 12. Then divide the group into pairs to work on the activity.

❖ Have the children take home their books to share page 13 and the *Preparing for Reconciliation* booklet 1. Encourage them to work on the *At Home* activity and booklet with their families.

❖ Ask the children to think of someone who might be a prayer partner to them. Have them complete the invitation on pages 75–76.

2 Following God's Law

Adult Background

The person who chooses to act immorally reveals that he or she is temporarily "stone deaf." When we look at the Latin roots of the word "obedience," we are reminded that it means "to hear." We show that we have heard God's commands by responding to them with loving and active compliance. Hearing, then, leads to the happiness of living in harmony with God's will.

By revealing the Ten Commandments to Moses on Mount Sinai, God clearly marked out a path of life. Those who remain on the path walk in freedom. The snares of sin (idolatry, disrespect for God or others, anger, infidelity, greed) cannot entangle them. When a rich young man asked Jesus how to gain eternal life, the Teacher responded, "If you wish to enter into life, keep the commandments" (Matthew 19:17).

Jesus came to fulfill the spirit of the Law. For Him, all the commandments are summed up as follows: "You shall love the Lord, your God, with all your heart, with all your soul, and with all your mind. You shall love your neighbor as yourself" (Matthew 22:37, 39).

Happy are we when our ears are open to these commands. And happy are those children with whom we share the true meaning of obedience.

Preparation Hints

In this session the commandments are taught as positive rules that guide us in making right choices. Familiarize the children with specific ways of carrying out these commandments in their own lives. Explain to them that God's laws are for our well-being and happiness—not just as individuals but as a whole community. Therefore, when God's laws are broken, all of us are hurt. While encouraging them to make right decisions, be sure the children understand that God never stops loving them, even when they have made bad choices.

Special-Needs Child

Treat mainstreamed children the same as other children. Expect the same standards of behavior.

Visual Needs
❖ preferential seating; closing activity in large type

Auditory Needs
❖ tape of Scripture story; headphones

Tactile-Motor Needs
❖ peer helper for cutout activity

Resources

Listen to the Maker Commandments in General (video)
Sacred Heart Kids' Club series
Don Bosco Multimedia
475 North Avenue, P.O. Box T
New Rochelle, NY 10802–0845
(1–800–342–5850)

God's Rules for Me (video)
St. Paul Books and Media
50 St. Paul's Avenue
Boston, MA 02130
(1–800–876–4463)

Materials for This Session
❖ Sadlier's *Songs: First Reconciliation* cassette or CD

Plan for the Session

Beginning ___ *min.*

❖ Make the sign of the cross prayerfully with the children.

❖ Ask the children to decide if the following "laws" are helpful or not:

• Play on the railroad tracks.

• Do not go to bed before midnight.

• Look both ways before crossing the street.

Go over these "laws," with the children. Then invite reponses to the opening three questions on page 14. Read together the six imaginary situations and share reactions. As a group, discuss the activity on page 15. Have the children share various rules that could appear on the signs. List these rules. Then have each child choose a rule from the list and write it under the appropriate picture.

Read the paragraph about God's laws. Emphasize that God's laws are given to us for our safety and happiness. Invite the children to pray the prayer together.

Middle ___ *min.*

❖ Ask the questions at the beginning of page 16 and allow time for the children to respond. Invite the children to look at the picture on page 17 as they listen to the Scripture story. Ask them why they think the law to love God and others is the greatest law of all.

Have the children then read the Law of Love several times to help them learn it by heart.

❖ Introduce the Ten Commandments by reading the first two paragraphs on page 18. Emphasize that these commandments are the laws God gave His people to help them love God and one another.

Introduce the word *sin* by reading the rest of the page. Review the children's understanding of the material by asking: "Does God stop loving us when we sin? When does God forgive us?"

❖ Go over the paraphrasing of the Ten Commandments on page 19. The commandments are expressed here in simple language to help the children understand how they affect their lives. If time allows, ask the children to provide examples of how we can keep each commandment. (The pictures illustrate some examples.)

❖ Introduce the children to the song "God Has Made Us a Family" on page 77. You might wish to use it at the group's First Reconciliation celebration.

End ___ *min.*

❖ Ask the children to recall as many commandments as they can. Have them look at page 19 for help. Then read the commandments together.

Go over the directions for the activity on page 20. Do the first sentence as a group and have the children explain their choices. Allow time for the children to complete the activity. Then, when all have finished, invite volunteers to share their responses. You might want to make this a group activity. Have the children make a face mask out of a paper plate. Have them show the happy or sad side as their response.

❖ Invite the children to bring their books to the prayer circle. Prepare in advance the children who will read each commandment. Encourage the group to respond reverently in prayer.

❖ Have the children take home their books to share page 21 and the *Preparing for Reconciliation* booklet 2. Encourage them to work on the *At Home* activity and booklet with their families.

3 Being Sorry, Being Forgiven

Adult Background

The word "contrition" comes from the Latin for "broken in spirit." We may experience this grace-prompted remorse for our sins as a softening of the heart or a breaking of stubborn willfulness. Like a gentle shower on parched earth, contrition restores the process of spiritual growth. It is the first step in preparing for sacramental Reconciliation.

Contrition is our response to the initial invitation of Jesus in Mark's good news: "Repent, and believe in the gospel" (1:15). It enables us to recognize that God's grace is greater than our sinfulness. It opens our hearts to the sincerity and truth in which holiness is rooted.

Children and adults alike need regular practice in saying "I'm sorry," and in validating their words with acts of recompense. Our daily reconciliations improve our cardiac health (physical and spiritual); they increase our capacity for a joyful celebration of the sacrament.

Preparation Hints

This session focuses on the importance of expressing sorrow for our sins—to God and to those whom our sins have hurt. Some children may find it more difficult than others to express sorrow. Encourage this expression by the dramatization of the story of the woman in Simon's house, creative play with puppets, or the use of some other artistic or musical medium. Lead the children to see that expressing sorrow for something wrong we have done brings us peace.

Special-Needs Child

Assign to the special-needs child a partner who is accepting of differences and can help the special-needs child with activities.

Visual Needs
❖ recordings of Scripture story and Act of Contrition

Auditory Needs
❖ preferential seating

Tactile-Motor Needs
❖ Act of Contrition taped to desk

Resources

Joey (video)
St. Paul Books and Media
50 St. Paul's Avenue
Boston, MA 02130
(1–800–876–4463)

Jesus Heals (video)
Jesus Stories series
EcuFilm
810 Twelfth Ave. So.
Nashville, TN 37203
(1–615–242–6277)

Materials for This Session

❖ Sadlier's *Songs: First Reconciliation* cassette

Plan for the Session

Beginning ___ min.

❖ Gather the children for prayer. Have the children repeat this prayer after you:

† Jesus, when we have done wrong, teach us how to be truly sorry.

❖ Explain to the children that they are going to finish some stories illustrated on pages 22–23. Read the first story and discuss how the story might end in forgiveness. List the children's ideas and have them choose an ending to write in their books. Do the same with the other two stories.

❖ Ask the closing question on page 23. Stress that saying "I'm sorry" is an important thing to do; even more important is to *show* we are sorry. Ask the children to suggest ways to do this.

Middle ___ min.

❖ Introduce the Scripture story by reading the first paragraph on page 24. Explain that in Palestine in Jesus' time, there were no paved roads. People's feet would get very dusty, so washing a guest's feet was a very hospitable thing to do.

Read the story and invite the children to examine the illustration on page 25. Review the story through these or similar questions: Did Simon welcome Jesus properly? Why or why not? What did Simon say about the woman? How did Jesus answer him?

Read the story again and have volunteers take the parts of Simon, Jesus, and the woman. Then ask the closing questions and have the group give examples of asking for forgiveness and forgiving others.

❖ Read the first paragraph on page 26. Point out that Jesus forgave the woman because she didn't just *say* she was sorry, she *showed* it. Display the word *reconciliation* and have the children find the meaning of this word in the next paragraph. Ask the children to tell how the pictures on pages 26–27 illustrate being reconciled.

Read the final two paragraphs asking the children to listen for the meaning of *contrition*.

❖ Go over, part by part, the Act of Contrition on page 27. Have the children note how the meaning of each part is summarized in the right-hand column. Have the children say the prayer several times together. Tell them that it is important to learn the prayer by heart.

❖ Introduce the children to the song "We Come to Ask Forgiveness" on page 77. You might wish to use it at the group's First Reconciliation celebration.

End ___ min.

❖ Have the children work with a partner to explain what happens in Reconciliation. Make sure they include the important points from paragraph four on page 26.

❖ Gather the children in a prayer circle. Read each question on page 28 slowly and invite the children to reflect quietly. It is important to respect their privacy, so do not call for shared responses. Encourage them to make a promise to ask (or to give) forgiveness of this person soon.

Go over the words and melody of the song with the children. Discuss what it means to be a disciple of Jesus, especially in connection with forgiveness.

❖ Have the children take home their books to share page 29 and the *Preparing for Reconciliation* booklet 3. Encourage them to work on the *At Home* activity and booklet with their families.

4 Examination of Conscience

Adult Background

In cartoons conscience is often depicted as a highly moral *alter ego* who contends against the devil's high-pressure sales tactics. When the *alter ego* says no to temptation, conscience wins another battle in the lifelong struggle to be accountable to God for our attitudes and actions.

Conscience in the Bible is visualized as "heart." The psalmist prays: "Probe me, God, know my heart. . . . See if my way is crooked" (Psalm 139:23, 24). To discover whether our way is crooked, we undertake a process of discernment known as an examination of conscience. Listening to the voice of God within us, we explore how faithful we have been to the dictates of our conscience, to the word of God, and to the teaching of the Church. Sin is a refusal to listen to a right conscience, and a failure to love.

God has many ways of probing our hearts. We can reflect on God's word in the liturgy, asking ourselves: How have I lived or failed to live this word? Does it reveal any sinful attitudes or habits I may have overlooked in the past?

Children can examine their hearts by asking: How have I shown my love for God and others? How have I failed to show love? (not praying, being disrespectful or dishonest, refusing to cooperate with others)

Preparation Hints

Help the children to understand that examination of conscience is a way of growing in our friendship with God. It is not just a preparation for Reconciliation; it should also be a part of our daily lives. Help them to see that Jesus wants us to do better each day, to discover what we need to change in order to follow Him more closely.

Take time to listen to the comments and responses of the children. In this way you will discover who needs help in discerning the consequences of their words and actions, and the value there is in recognizing and being sorry for unloving choices.

Special-Needs Child

When working with mainstreamed children, stress their strengths and help them assess their limitations realistically.

Visual Needs
❖ enlargement of questions on page 35

Auditory Needs
❖ headphones for music

Tactile-Motor Needs
❖ examination of conscience questions taped to desk

Resources

Skateboard (video)
Mass Media Ministries
2116 North Charles Street
Baltimore, MD 21218
(1–800–828–8825)

Keep Love Alive (video)
Sacred Heart Kids' Club, series III
Don Bosco Multimedia
475 North Avenue, P.O. Box T
New Rochelle, NY 10802–0845
(1–800–342–5850)

Materials for This Session

❖ Sadlier's *Songs: First Reconciliation* cassette or CD

Plan for the Session

Beginning ___ min.

❖ Begin the session by telling the children that God loves all of us and asks us to welcome and love one another. Go over the directions for the opening activity, then introduce the melody and words of the song. Gather the children in a "love ring" to do the activity.

❖ Read the first paragraph on page 31. Discuss the group's responses to the questions about ways to make good choices. Then encourage each child to make up a prayer to the Holy Spirit for guidance, and to share it. Read the last paragraph to introduce the Scripture story.

Middle ___ min.

❖ Ask the children what a shepherd is and does. Stress that a shepherd's work is to protect and care for the sheep. Then ask: "What if you had one hundred sheep and one of them was lost, what would you do?"

❖ Invite the children to look at the picture on page 33 as you read the Scripture story. Point out that the shepherd is full of joy because he has found the lost sheep. Stress that Jesus tells us He is full of joy when someone who has done wrong is truly sorry.

❖ Read the first two paragraphs on page 34. Introduce the word *conscience*. Point out that, unlike sheep, we have the ability to know right from wrong. Invite volunteers to tell of times in their own lives when they knew what was right and what was wrong.

❖ Read the next two paragraphs introducing *examination of conscience*. Explain that when we "examine" something we look at it carefully. When we examine our consciences we think carefully about our choices. Children at this age should simply ask themselves about the things they have done wrong and the good things they could have done, but did not. Point out that we should ask ourselves if we have been living as Jesus wants.

❖ Go over the suggested questions on page 35 (based on the Ten Commandments) to help the children examine their choices. Invite them to ask the Holy Spirit to help them. Then slowly read each question, allowing time for personal reflection after each one. Note: these questions are to be answered silently, and are not to be shared aloud.

Encourage the children to use this page to examine their consciences as their immediate preparation for the sacrament of Reconciliation.

You might wish at this time to call the children's attention to pages 71–72. Point out the prayers that are listed and encourage the children to pray them each day.

End ___ min.

❖ Invite the children to act out the story of the lost sheep. Guide the dramatization by using the direction and question in the first paragraph on page 36.

❖ Have the children listen to the song, "Always Ready to Forgive." Discuss the relationship of this song with the Bible story. Go over the words and then sing it together to end the session.

❖ Have the children take home their books to share page 37 and the *Preparing for Reconciliation* booklet 4. Encourage them to work on the *At Home* activity and booklet with their families.

5 Celebrating Reconciliation

Adult Background

It is the sacrament of many names. Yet each name contributes to our understanding of this healing encounter with the divine Physician. The Church calls it the sacrament of:

- Penance (repentance and satisfaction for sin);
- conversion (turning back to God);
- confession (confronting our sin);
- forgiveness (absolution);
- Reconciliation (healing and restoring relationships).

(See *Catechism of the Catholic Church*, 1423–1424.)

The benefits of the sacrament are many: renewed spiritual strength, remission of sin, interior peace and consolation, unity with Christ and His Church. For those who celebrate Reconciliation with sincere hearts, there is the great joy of the paralytic to whom Jesus said, "Courage, child, your sins are forgiven" (Matthew 9:2).

By our own eager and prayerful preparation for Reconciliation, we encourage children to desire this joyful encounter with Jesus. In it He gives us His peace and makes us His ambassadors of peace to others.

Preparation Hints

To allay any worries the children might have regarding the celebration of the individual rite, plan a visit to the reconciliation room in the parish church. Invite the parents to be part of this visit. To make sure the room is arranged correctly, you may need to check it in advance.

Special-Needs Child

When pairing the group members for activities, assign the mainstreamed children a partner who is both accepting of differences and a capable helper.

Visual Needs
❖ enlarged copies of the gospel play

Auditory Needs
❖ headphones for music

Tactile-Motor Needs
❖ large word cards for *Reconciliation*, *confession*, and *absolution*

Resources

First Reconciliation (video)
St. Anthony Messenger and Franciscan Communications
1615 Republic Street
Cincinnati, OH 45210
(1–800–488–0488)

Materials for This Session

❖ Sadlier's *Songs: First Reconciliation* cassette or CD

Plan for the Session

Beginning ___ min.

❖ This session begins with a gospel-play (pages 38–39). Point out that in Jesus' day many tax collectors were dishonest.

After going over the story, practice the song on page 39. Then assign children to their parts in the play. Invite the children to act out the gospel story.

Discuss the closing questions with the children. Emphasize how Zacchaeus reconciles with Jesus and also with the community. Help the children see that Jesus *wants* to bring us joy, forgiveness, and peace.

Middle ___ min.

❖ Read the two paragraphs on page 40. Stress that we celebrate God's forgiveness and peace when we celebrate the sacrament of Reconciliation.

Call attention to the photographs on pages 40–41. As a group activity, make a story or play about forgiveness and reconciliation for each picture.

❖ The first two paragraphs on page 41 introduce the two rites, or ways we can celebrate the sacrament. Point out that in each rite we tell our sins to the priest. Emphasize that the priest never reveals what he is told in confession. Then read together the closing paragraph.

❖ For the next part of the session, arrange a special setting to simulate the reconciliation room in church.

Emphasize the availability of a screen (with a kneeler) for anyone who feels more comfortable talking to the priest without seeing him face-to-face.

❖ Have the children turn to the *Individual Rite of Reconciliation* on page 42. Emphasize that when we examine our conscience (see page 35) we ask ourselves if we have been living as Jesus wants.

Have the children follow along as you read each of the steps. Review the Act of Contrition (see page 27).

❖ Have the children look at the pictures on pages 42–43. Call on volunteers to identify the step that is shown in each picture. Display the word *absolution*.

❖ Have the children turn to page 44. Explain that at special times of the year we also celebrate Reconciliation with the members of our parish family. Read the steps that tell how we celebrate the sacrament with others. Ask volunteers to identify the steps that each person does with the priest alone.

❖ Go over the steps on page 45 that are always part of the sacrament of Reconciliation.

End ___ min.

❖ Set aside time to visit the reconciliation room in church. Call attention to the photos on page 46. Ask the children what is different about each way to receive the sacrament. As the children share their thoughts on celebrating the sacrament, be reassuring and supportive. Then ask the children to offer their ideas on ways to prepare for this sacrament.

❖ Have the children cut out the heart in the back of the book. You may wish to have the children wear these when they celebrate First Reconciliation as a simple reminder of Jesus' never-ending love.

Introduce the children to the song "New Hope" on page 78. You might use it at the group's First Reconciliation celebration.

❖ Have the children take home their books to share page 47 and the *Preparing for Reconciliation* booklet 5. Encourage them to work on the *At Home* activity and booklet with their families.

6 Living As Peacemakers

Adult Background

What we have received as a gift in Reconciliation we are called to give to others. Jesus says to those who have been restored to unity in the Body of Christ, "Peace I leave with you; my peace I give to you" (John 14:27). As we have been forgiven, so we go forth to forgive, to reconcile, and to teach peace. The Scripture writer promises, "Those who counsel peace have joy" (Proverbs 12:20).

The biblical concept of *shalom* encompasses a broader blessing than does our English word "peace." It implies that we have all that we need and that our relationships (with God and neighbor) are harmonious. It describes a lasting communion with Jesus and His Church. "For he is our peace, he who made both one and broke down the dividing wall of enmity" (Ephesians 2:14).

As ministers of reconciliation and peace, we look to Jesus and the saints for guidance. Catherine of Siena worked to bring enemies within the Church together. Elizabeth of Portugal did the same with political factions. Francis Xavier and Martin de Porres ministered to those divided by racial and cultural differences. Francis of Assisi made peace between persons, communities, and with all creation. When we follow in their grace-filled footprints, we share the peace we have been given. (See Isaiah 52:7.)

Preparation Hints

Help the children to understand that their celebration of the sacrament does not end with First Reconciliation. Jesus sends them out to live God's Law of Love, to forgive others, and to be signs of peace and justice in the world.

Encourage the children to form a deeper relationship with Jesus and the community by praying often, helping others, and being peacemakers. Discuss with the children their hopes for peace in our world. Guide them to suggest ways they can contribute to that peace.

Special-Needs Child

Special-needs children may have difficulty concentrating. Involve them in helping you throughout the lesson.

Visual Needs
❖ enlargement of "Prayer of Saint Francis"

Auditory Needs
❖ clear, concise directions

Tactile-Motor Needs
❖ peers to assist with activities

Resources

Saint Francis of Assisi (video)
Saints Alive series
William H. Sadlier, Inc.
9 Pine Street
New York, NY 10005–1002
1–800–221–5175

Materials for This Session

❖ Sadlier's *Songs: First Reconciliation* cassette or CD

Plan for the Session

NOTE: This session is shorter than the others. Schedule activities accordingly.

Beginning ___ min.

❖ Have music playing softly as the children enter. Then quietly gather the children in a circle. As you read the Scripture story with expression and feeling, invite the children to look at the illustration on page 49.

❖ Have the children share what they liked best about the story and picture. Ask the children to use their imaginations as you read the last paragraph on page 48. Read the questions in a gentle, meditative style. Direct the children to answer the questions in the quiet of their hearts. Afterwards, those who wish may share their answers.

Middle ___ min.

❖ Read aloud the first paragraph on page 50. Invite the children to talk about when we should celebrate Reconciliation. (Note: Tell the children that the sacrament is always available to them in the Church whenever they need it.) Continue reading the rest of the page. Emphasize that the sacrament of Reconciliation makes a difference in our lives. It is a sign that we are growing as friends of Jesus and that we are called to give God's peace to others.

❖ Call attention to the chart on page 51. Invite the children to give examples of how we can live as God's peacemakers, using the list as a guide. Then ask the children to describe how the pictures on these pages show various ways of sharing peace.

❖ You might wish to take a few minutes to go over the directions for "A Peacemaker Checklist" on pages 73–74. Explain to the children that they will complete this activity at home with their family members.

End ___ min.

❖ Read the question at the top of page 52. Invite the children to share their ideas. Then call attention to the picture on this page. Ask them if they can identify this person. Explain that St. Francis tried to be as much like Jesus as he possibly could. Most of all, he wanted to be a peacemaker like Jesus.

❖ Read aloud the introductory paragraph. Then invite the children to read along with you the *Prayer of Saint Francis*. Take each line of the prayer and ask the children to suggest ways they might bring love, pardon, faith, hope, light, and joy to people who lack these gifts.

❖ Suggest gestures to go with each line of the prayer. For example:

line 1: arms extended up CHANGE TO arms crossed over chest

line 2: clenched fists CHANGE TO hands on heart

line 3: right fist clenched, right arm swung out to side stiffly CHANGE TO two short taps on heart with right fist

line 4: arms hanging at sides CHANGE TO hands folded in prayer

line 5: arm across eyes CHANGES TO hands at chin level with palms facing up

line 6: hands over closed eyes CHANGE TO eyes looking up with hands cupping chin

line 7: head bowed, arms at sides CHANGE TO head uplifted, arms raised high

Practice the gestures, then pray the prayer together to end the session.

❖ Introduce the children to the song "Peace to You and Me" on page 78. You might wish to use it at the group's First Reconciliation celebration.

❖ Have the children take home their books to share page 53 and the *Preparing for Reconciliation* booklet 6. Encourage them to work on the *At Home* activity and booklet with their families.

A Peacemaking Rite

Purpose

Just as the time of preparation began with a celebratory rite in the presence of the parish assembly, so too does it close with this *Peacemaking Rite*. Again, the parents (or guardians) of the children participate in solemnly recognizing the important step the children have taken in their sacramental and spiritual lives. The rite, taking place within the heart of the community, reaffirms for the children the reconciling presence of Jesus in their lives and sends them forth to be His peacemakers. The children are given their First Reconciliation certificates.

Scheduling the Rite

An appropriate time for this rite is within the liturgy for a regularly scheduled parish Mass the weekend following their celebration of Reconciliation. The rite takes place just before the final blessing of the Mass. Talk with the pastor about scheduling the *Peacemaking Rite* within the parish Sunday (or Saturday evening) Mass. Copies of the rite should be given to the pastor and to the celebrant of the Mass. Adapt the rite to the number of children involved and to the constraints and possibilities of your parish church. For example, you might wish to seat the parents *beside* their child for this rite.

Involvement of the Parish Community

It is important that the presiding priest or the catechist give the assembly a *brief* introduction to the meaning and purpose of the rite, inviting the community to participate and to sing the closing hymn.

Parent/Guardian Involvement

Make sure the parents or guardians are fully informed by letter as to their participation in the rite. A follow-up reminder call would be helpful as well. Ask the parents to come to Mass a little early so that you can arrange seating and go over the rite together.

Preparation with the Children

❖ Go over the rite with the children. Explain that their families and their parish community want to support and pray for them in this important step they have taken in their life of faith.

❖ Have the children look at the certificate in the back of their books. Read it together. Then have them carefully remove it. Collect the certificates.

❖ Go over the closing song. Have the children listen to the music on the cassette a few times and then sing along with it.

❖ Make sure to communicate with parents or guardians, informing them of all the details of the Mass, including the rite. Have extra copies of the rite available at the Mass.

Suggestions for Families

It is in the home that children learn by their experiences of forgiving and being forgiven. When does reconciliation take place in the home? How does the family celebrate reconciliation?

❖ Take time to review the lesson your child has finished. Read over the *Family Focus* note. Your enthusiam will enhance your child's interest in doing the home activity with you.

❖ Ask your child why he or she does certain actions. Ask the question about good actions as well as bad actions. Celebrating the "good" helps a child discover how pleasing it is to be good.

❖ Encourage your child, in a story-telling form, to talk about the day at school or at home, mentioning good and bad things that happened. Finding the "why" in these things helps the child form his or her conscience. Then guide the child about ways to change actions and behaviors depending on the answer to "why."

❖ Take advantage of opportunities to discuss with your child how to reconcile when reconciliation is needed. Find ways to celebrate that reconciliation—for example, a special cake, playing a favorite game together.

❖ Give your child a respect for law. When you set rules for the family, be consistent in their applications. Children become confused when rules are sometimes enforced, sometimes overlooked. If an exception is made to a rule, be sure to explain why.

❖ Offer your child choices whenever you can. Let him or her discover the consequence of the choice—then talk about it.

❖ Imitate Jesus: make sure your child knows he or she is loved even when something wrong has been done. For example: "I love you, but I don't like the way you treated your sister."

❖ Encourage your child to say "I'm sorry" if he or she is sorry. For example, say: "If you feel badly that you threw that toy at Peter, you can tell him."

❖ When you have done something for which you are sorry, let your children hear you say the words to whomever you have hurt.

❖ Model the spirit of reconciliation by your own behavior toward neighbors and friends. Talk with your child about ways to handle conflict: by talking calmly and listening respectfully.

❖ What is your attitude toward those who ask you to change? With your child, talk about the importance of learning how to accept and to grow from constructive criticism.

❖ Make time to listen and to share with your child. This undivided attention builds feelings of self-worth.

❖ Have family members write a note to Jesus about experiences within the family that have hurt. Come together and burn the notes as a sign of the healing that you ask of Jesus. Then celebrate together in a special way.

❖ Plan an "act of kindness" day in which the whole family participates. At the end of the day talk about what each has done.

❖ Encourage the celebration of the sacrament of Reconciliation regularly as a way for family members to grow in the Christian life.

Sadlier Sacrament Program
With You Always

First Reconciliation

Dr. Gerard F. Baumbach
Moya Gullage

Rev. Msgr. John F. Barry
Dr. Eleanor Ann Brownell
Helen Hemmer, I.H.M.
Dr. Norman F. Josaitis
Rev. Michael J. Lanning, O.F.M.
Dr. Marie Murphy
Karen Ryan
Joseph F. Sweeney

Official Theological Consultant
Most Rev. Edward K. Braxton, Ph. D., S.T.D.

Pastoral Consultant
Rev. Virgilio P. Elizondo, Ph. D., S.T.D.

Catechetical and Liturgical Consultants
Dr. Gerard F. Baumbach
Dr. Eleanor Ann Brownell

with
Dr. Thomas H. Groome
Boston College

William H. Sadlier, Inc.
9 Pine Street
New York, NY 10005-1002

Nihil Obstat

✠ Most Reverend George O. Wirz

Censor Librorum

Imprimatur

✠ Most Reverend William H. Bullock

Bishop of Madison

July 10, 1995

Home Office: 9 Pine Street
New York, NY 10005–1002
ISBN: 0–8215–2401–1
  56789/987

Acknowledgments

Excerpts and adaptations from *Good News Bible*, copyright © American Bible Society 1966, 1971, 1976, 1979.

Excerpts from the English translation of *Rite of Penance* © 1974, International Committee on English in the Liturgy, Inc. (ICEL). All rights reserved.

"Always Ready to Forgive," © 1990, Carey Landry and North American Liturgy Resources (NALR). All rights reserved. "Let There Be Peace on Earth," © renewed 1983, 1955, Jan-Lee Music, Honokaa, Hawaii. All rights reserved. "God Has Made Us a Family," © 1986, Carey Landry and North American Liturgy Resources (NALR). All rights reserved. "We Come to Ask Forgiveness," © 1986, Carey Landry and North American Liturgy Resources. All rights reserved. "New Hope," © 1976, North American Liturgy Resources (NALR), 5536 NE Hassalo, Portland, OR 97213. All rights reserved. Used with permission. "Peace to You and Me," © 1986, Carey Landry and North American Liturgy Resources (NALR). All rights reserved.

Photo Credits

Jim Saylor — Photo Editor

Mary Kate Coudal — Photo Research

Cate Photography: 4, 5, 6, 7, 10, 11 right, 14, 15 top right, 18, 19 bottom, 21, 26, 34, 35, 42, 43, 46, 50–51, 54, 55.
CROSIERS/ Gene Plaisted, OSC: 18/19, 44/45.
Kathy Ferguson: 15 top left.
James Frank: 41 top.
Gerald French/ FPG International: 15 bottom.
Ken Karp: 11 left, 12, 20, 22, 23, 27, 28, 30/31, 31, 36.
H. Armstrong Roberts: 76 center.
Tony Stone Images/ Lori Adamski Peek: 19 top; Dan Bosler: 40 left; Ken Fisher: 76 top left, 76 bottom right; Bruce Aryes: 76 top right; Peter Correz: 76 bottom left.
Rod Walker: 41 bottom.
George White: 40 right.

Illustrators

Bonnie Matthews: 3, 4–8, 10–12, 14–16, 18–20, 22–24, 26–28, 30–32, 34–38, 40–46, 48, 50–51, 54–79

Robert VanNutt: 9, 17, 25, 33, 38–39, 49, 52, 57, 59, 61, 63, 65, 67, Jesus cutout

Michael Woo: 21, 29, 47, 53, pinwheel cutout

Contents

A Preparation Rite

Leader: Jesus says, "I am the Good Shepherd. I know My sheep and they know Me."

Based on John 10:15

All: (To the tune of "Did You Ever See A Lassie?")
♫ Oh, Jesus is our Friend, and our
    Brother and Shepherd.
Jesus teaches us to love and to
    follow His way.
In joy and in faith and in hope and
    thanksgiving,
Jesus teaches us to love and to
    follow His way. ♫

Leader: As a parish family, we welcome you as you begin to prepare for the sacrament of Reconciliation. We join with you as you get ready to celebrate God's great love and mercy. As followers of Jesus, the Good Shepherd, we help each other by praying:

Leader: Jesus, help us to grow in faith and trust.

All: Jesus, Good Shepherd, hear us.

Leader: Jesus, help us to love and follow You.

All: Jesus, Good Shepherd, hear us.

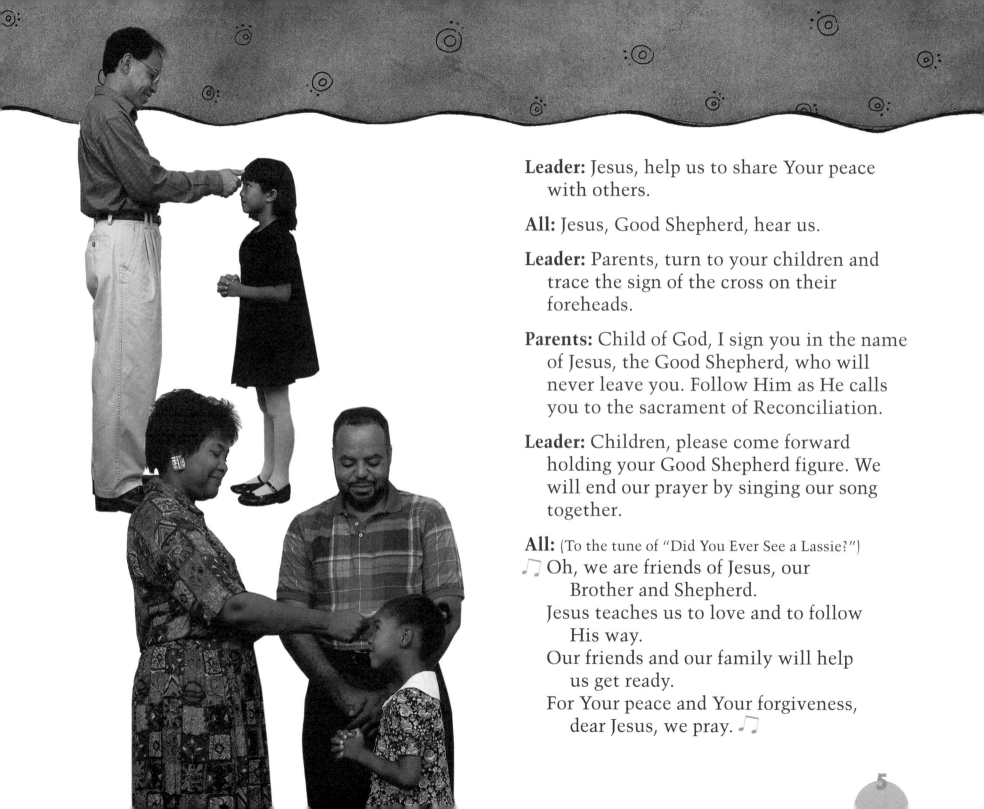

Leader: Jesus, help us to share Your peace with others.

All: Jesus, Good Shepherd, hear us.

Leader: Parents, turn to your children and trace the sign of the cross on their foreheads.

Parents: Child of God, I sign you in the name of Jesus, the Good Shepherd, who will never leave you. Follow Him as He calls you to the sacrament of Reconciliation.

Leader: Children, please come forward holding your Good Shepherd figure. We will end our prayer by singing our song together.

All: (To the tune of "Did You Ever See a Lassie?")
♫ Oh, we are friends of Jesus, our
  Brother and Shepherd.
Jesus teaches us to love and to follow
  His way.
Our friends and our family will help
  us get ready.
For Your peace and Your forgiveness,
  dear Jesus, we pray. ♫

5

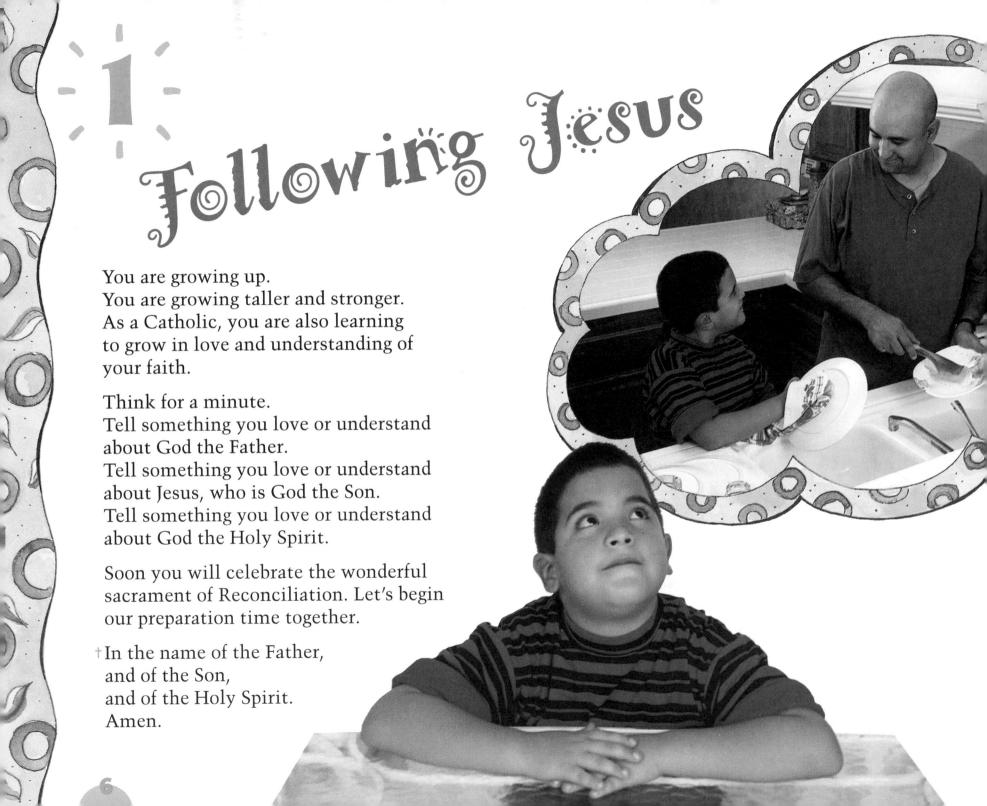

1 Following Jesus

You are growing up.
You are growing taller and stronger.
As a Catholic, you are also learning to grow in love and understanding of your faith.

Think for a minute.
Tell something you love or understand about God the Father.
Tell something you love or understand about Jesus, who is God the Son.
Tell something you love or understand about God the Holy Spirit.

Soon you will celebrate the wonderful sacrament of Reconciliation. Let's begin our preparation time together.

† In the name of the Father,
and of the Son,
and of the Holy Spirit.
Amen.

How wonderful God is!
He gives us so many gifts — our families,
our friends, our Church, our wonderful world!
Tell about some of God's best gifts to you.

God also gives us the gift of choice.
Choices are things we do on purpose.
We are free to choose to do what is right.
We can also choose to do what is wrong.

What are some of the choices God wants
us to make?

Today we are going to hear a story from the
Bible about someone who first made a wrong
choice and then made a right choice!

The Forgiving Father

There was a loving father who had two sons. One day the younger son said to his father:

"Father, give me my share of the family money." He wanted to leave home and have some fun.

The father was very sad but he gave his son the money and watched him leave home.

At first the young man had a wonderful time. He gave parties and made many new friends. Soon, however, his money was gone. His friends left him. He was poor and homeless and hungry.

Now he began to think about the choice he had made. The son remembered his home and his father's great love for him!

The young man said:

"I will go home to my father. I will say, 'Father, I have sinned against God and against you. I am not fit to be your son. Treat me as one of your servants.'"

Then he began his long trip home.

His father kept hoping that one day his son would return. Each day he watched and waited. When he saw his son coming down the road, he ran to meet him and hugged him. Then the father said to his servants:

"Put the best robe on my son and new shoes on his feet. Now we will celebrate, for my son who was dead is alive again. He was lost, but now he's found!"

Based on Luke 15:11–24

What wrong choice did the son make?
What right choice did he make?
What choices did the father make?
What do you learn from this story about God's great love for us?

Making Loving Choices

Jesus showed us how to make good and loving choices. He was kind to others. He healed the sick. He forgave sins. He brought people peace. He taught us that love is the most important thing of all.

It is not always easy to make right and loving choices.

We should always begin by asking God to help us make the right choice in following Jesus. Then, if what we have to choose is hard or something serious, we need to talk about it with someone we trust — a parent or another grown-up. Then, with the help of the Holy Spirit, we choose the right and loving thing to do.

Sometimes what we do may cause a problem. We may make a mistake. We may do something by accident. Then it is not our fault. Mistakes and accidents are not sins.

How can you show you are Jesus' follower? How can you make loving choices?

How to Make a Loving Choice

1. Think about the choices you can make.

2. Ask yourself which choice Jesus would want you to make.

3. Talk to God about your choices. Ask the Holy Spirit to help you to choose to do right and loving things as Jesus did.

4. Talk over your choices with someone who can help you.

5. With the help of the Holy Spirit, make your choice.

What Is a Choice?

Read these stories. Work with a partner and label them W (a wrong choice), R (a right choice), A (an accident), or M (a mistake). Explain your answers.

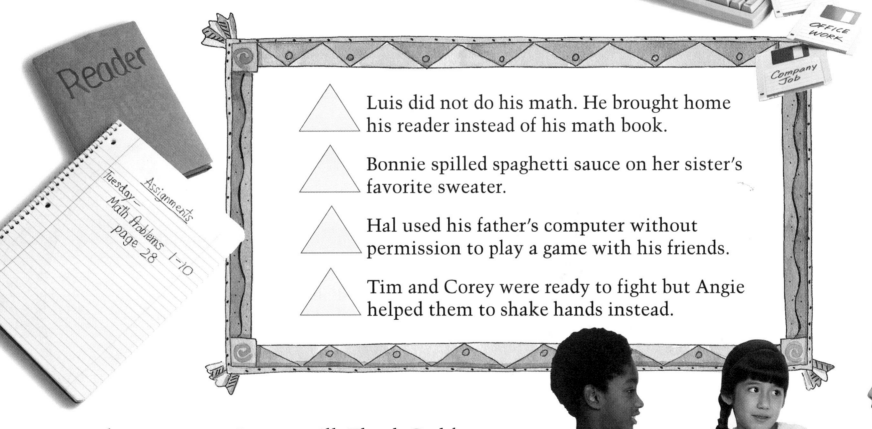

△ Luis did not do his math. He brought home his reader instead of his math book.

△ Bonnie spilled spaghetti sauce on her sister's favorite sweater.

△ Hal used his father's computer without permission to play a game with his friends.

△ Tim and Corey were ready to fight but Angie helped them to shake hands instead.

Close your eyes. Be very still. Thank God for giving you the freedom to make choices. Ask God to help you to make loving choices that Jesus wants His friends to make.

At Home

Throughout this preparation time for the sacrament of Reconciliation, emphasize with your child that Reconciliation is a wonderful sacrament of God's loving forgiveness, joy, and peace. It is important that you try to give your child a very positive attitude toward this sacrament from the very beginning. Lesson One focuses on the freedom God gives us to choose and how we learn to make loving choices.

1. Read through the lesson together. Let your child tell you about the story of the lost son and the choices he made. Point out that God is like the father in the story who always loves and forgives us when we are sorry.

2. Sometimes we have to make hard choices. Go over the steps in this kind of decision making with your child. Assure your child that you will always be there to help with the hard choices.

3. Stress that our choices—right or wrong—are things we deliberately do on purpose. Accidents and mistakes are not choices we make to disobey God; therefore they are not sins. See whether your child understands this principle by going over the activity on page 12.

Write the letter that matches each colored shape.

A	C	D	E	G	H	I	K	L	M	N	O	P	S	T	V	Y
●	■	▲	▬	◆	▼	●	■	▲	▬	◆	▼	●	■	▲	▬	◆

1. We learn to C __ __ __ __ __ right from wrong.

2. We should ask God to __ __ __ __ us.

3. We want to choose __ __ __ __ __ __ things to do as Jesus did.

4. Sometimes we make __ __ __ __ __ __ __ __ .

5. We may do something by __ __ __ __ __ __ __ __ .

6. It is not always __ __ __ __ to choose to love like Jesus.

Now write the letters from the ◯s above to complete this sentence.

God gives us the gift of ◯ ◯ ◯ ◯ ◯ ◯ .

         1   2   3   4   5   6

How will you use God's gift today?

2 Following God's Law

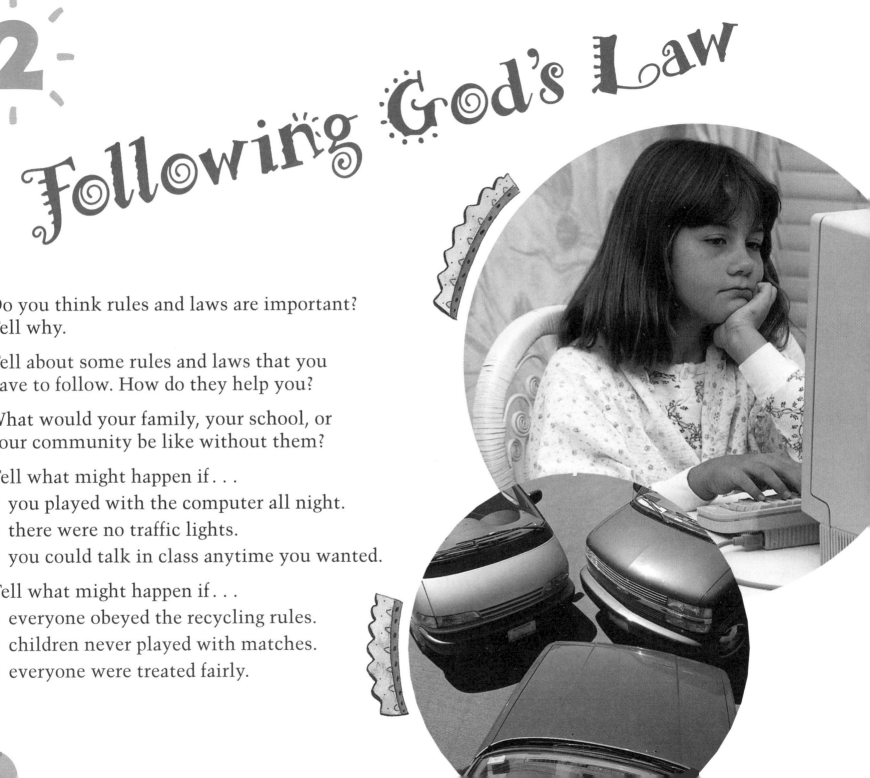

Do you think rules and laws are important? Tell why.

Tell about some rules and laws that you have to follow. How do they help you?

What would your family, your school, or your community be like without them?

Tell what might happen if...
* you played with the computer all night.
* there were no traffic lights.
* you could talk in class anytime you wanted.

Tell what might happen if...
* everyone obeyed the recycling rules.
* children never played with matches.
* everyone were treated fairly.

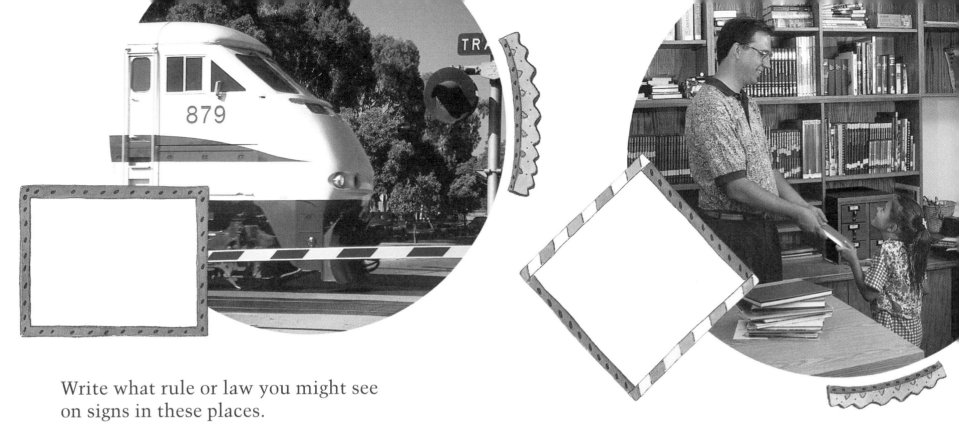

Write what rule or law you might see
on signs in these places.

- at a railroad crossing
- in a library
- at a zoo park

Tell why these are good rules.

Because God loves us so much, He gives
us laws to help us. Why do God's people
need rules and laws? Share your ideas.

Let's pray.

†Dear God, teach us Your law.
Help us to follow it.

The Most Important Law

What if someone asked you to name the most important law of all?
What would you say?

One day someone asked Jesus just that question.

"Teacher," he said to Jesus, "which is the greatest commandment that God gave us?"

Jesus answered,

"The greatest commandment is this:
Love the Lord your God with all your heart, with all your soul, and with all your mind.
Love your neighbor as you love yourself."

Based on Matthew 22: 35–39

We call this greatest commandment the Law of Love.

Jesus said that the most important law is love — love of God, love of others, and love of ourselves. When we obey this great Law of Love, we do what God wants us to do.

Let's say the Law of Love together.
Can you learn it by heart?

God's Law

We show that we love God, others, and ourselves when we follow the Ten Commandments. They help us to live the Law of Love, as Jesus did.

The Ten Commandments tell us how God wants us to show our love. Sometimes people choose not to follow God's law. They turn away from God's love. They sin.

Sin is freely choosing to do what we know to be wrong. It means disobeying God's law on purpose. All sins are wrong.

Sin hurts us and hurts the members of God's family, too. When we sin, we choose not to love God or others or ourselves. Even when we sin, God does not stop loving us. God always forgives us when we are sorry and try not to sin again.

Look at page 19 to learn how the Ten Commandments teach us to love as God wants.

Third Commandment

Fifth Commandment

Fourth Commandment

Living the Ten Commandments

We show we love God when:

1. We think first of what God wants when we make choices.

2. We use God's name only with love and respect.

3. We keep Sunday as God's special day of prayer and rest.

We show we love ourselves and others when:

4. We listen to and obey those who care for us.

5. We care for all living things.

6. We respect our own bodies and the bodies of others.

7. We do not take anything that is not ours; we are fair to everyone.

8. We are truthful in what we say and do.

9. We are faithful to those we love.

10. We help people to have what they need to live.

Doing What God Wants

Draw a 🙂 beside the sentences that tell how to follow God's commandments.

Draw a ☹ beside the sentences that do not tell about following God's laws.

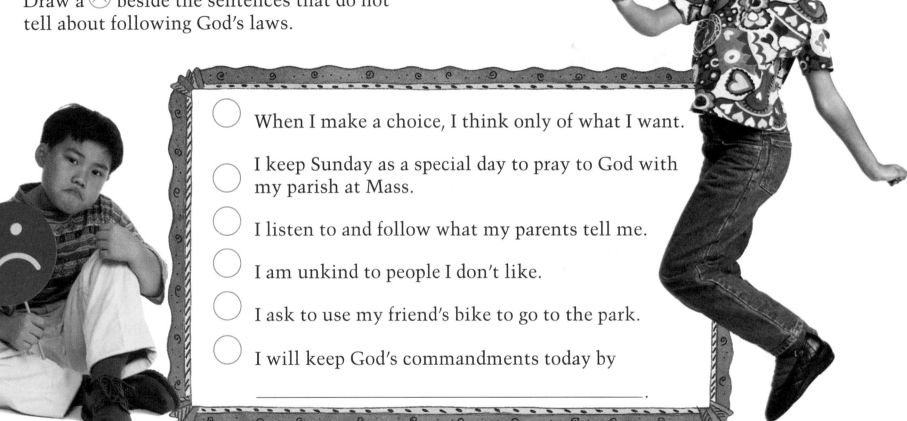

○ When I make a choice, I think only of what I want.

○ I keep Sunday as a special day to pray to God with my parish at Mass.

○ I listen to and follow what my parents tell me.

○ I am unkind to people I don't like.

○ I ask to use my friend's bike to go to the park.

○ I will keep God's commandments today by

_____.

Gather in a prayer circle. Have ten people read in turn one of the sentences on page 19. After each one, pray together:

† Loving God, help us to do what is right.

Family Focus

In this lesson your child explored the Law of Love and the Ten Commandments as the laws God has given us to help us live as He wants us to live. You might want to begin by discussing together some family rules and how they help your family. Then talk about God's laws. Emphasize that God gives us laws to help us live healthy and happy lives.

Note that the Ten Commandments themselves are not given. The children are taught how to live the commandments. They are worded in such a way that young children can understand and relate to them. If you wish to review the commandments, see page 19. (You can find the scriptural wording in Exodus 20:1–17.)

1. Have your child tell you the gospel story of the greatest commandment. Go over the Law of Love together. Then go over the explanations of the Ten Commandments on page 19.

2. Help your child understand that sin is a free choice to do what we know is wrong. We cannot sin if we do not choose to do so. Make sure your child knows that God always forgives us when we are sorry.

3. Do the **At Home** activity together.

Talk with your family about the ways you will try to live the Law of Love this week.

Cut out the Law of Love pinwheel in the back of the book.

Read the message on the pinwheel. Share it with your family. Then use the pinwheel as a centerpiece for your family table.

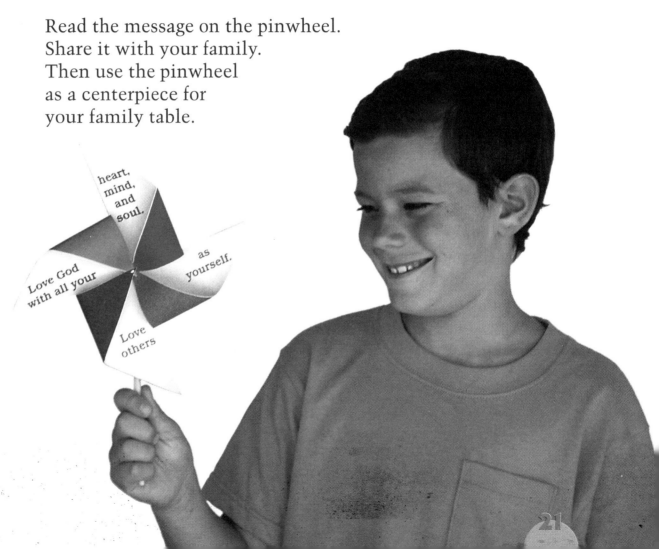

3

Being Sorry, Being Forgiven

How would you end each story?
Share with your group.

Ben and Tony had a fight. They called
each other bad names. They wanted
to hurt each other. Tony's big brother
pulled them apart. "Calm down," he
said. "This is no way to settle things."
Ben and Tony took deep breaths.
They calmed down. Then they

_____

_____

Laura received a new computer game for her birthday. She brought it to school to show her friends. When Mark saw it, he was jealous. He had wanted one like that for a long time. So he grabbed the game and threw it. Then this is what Mark did.

_____

_____

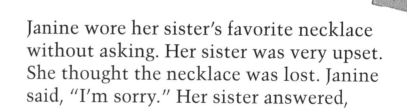

Janine wore her sister's favorite necklace without asking. Her sister was very upset. She thought the necklace was lost. Janine said, "I'm sorry." Her sister answered,

_____

_____

What do you think God wants us to do when we do something wrong?

The One Who Was Forgiven

In Jesus' time people wore sandals. The roads were very dusty. When guests were invited to someone's house, the host would have a servant wash their feet with water to make them feel comfortable. It was an act of welcome, of courtesy.

One day, Simon, an important man in town, invited Jesus to his house for dinner. Simon, however, did not welcome Jesus with courtesy. He did not offer Jesus water to have His feet washed.

During the dinner, a woman who had committed many sins came in. She knelt at Jesus' feet. She cried so hard that her tears washed the dust from His feet. She wanted Jesus to know how sorry she was for her sins.

Simon was very angry. He said to Jesus, "Don't you know this woman? She is a sinner. You shouldn't let her be near you!"

Jesus said, "Simon, when I came to your house, you gave me no water for my feet. This woman has washed my feet with her tears. I tell you, Simon, all her sins have been forgiven because of her great love."

Then He said to the woman, "Your sins are forgiven. Go in peace."
Based on Luke 7:36–40, 44–50

Why did Jesus forgive the woman?
What do you think Jesus wants us to do when we have done something wrong?
What does Jesus want us to do when someone does something wrong to us? Why?

Being Sorry, Being Reconciled

Jesus knew that the woman was sorry for all her sins. Jesus understands when we are sorry, too. Like the woman, we will be forgiven, no matter what we have done, when we are sorry.

Sometimes it is not enough just to say "I'm sorry." Being sorry also means wanting to make up, or to be reconciled, with those we have hurt. It means trying not to sin again.

Reconciliation is the sacrament in which we celebrate God's mercy and forgiveness of our sins.

When we celebrate the sacrament of Reconciliation, we tell God that we are sorry for what we have done wrong. We promise not to sin again and to try to make things right. God always forgives us.

We say a special prayer of sorrow when we celebrate Reconciliation. It is called an Act of Contrition. Contrition is sorrow for sin.

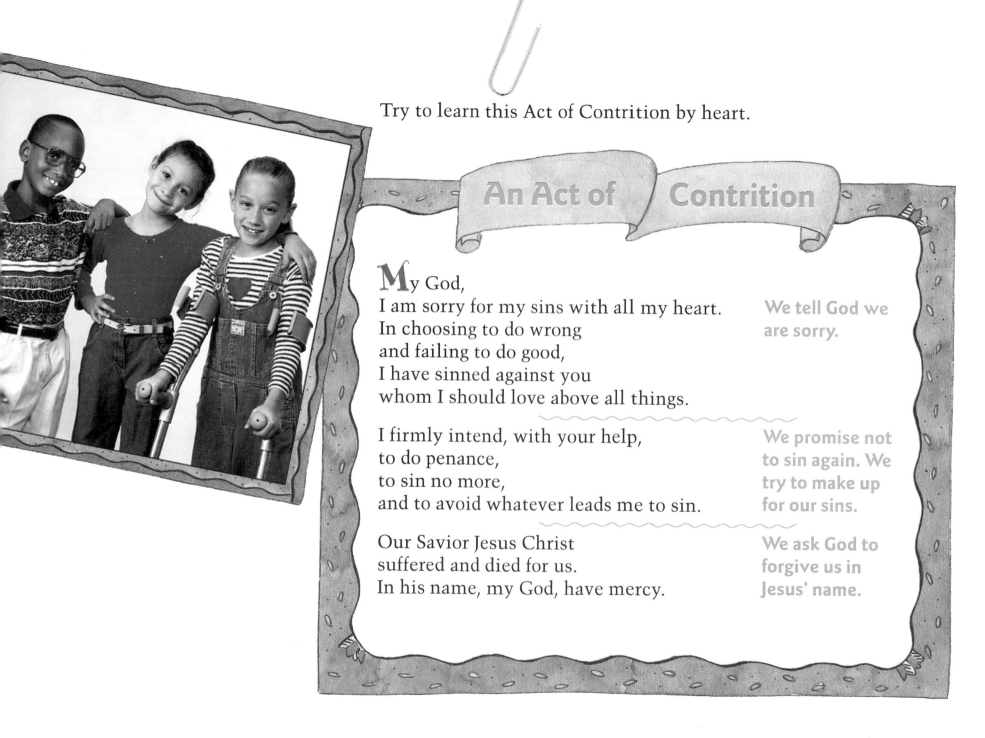

Try to learn this Act of Contrition by heart.

An Act of Contrition

My God,
I am sorry for my sins with all my heart.
In choosing to do wrong
and failing to do good,
I have sinned against you
whom I should love above all things.

We tell God we are sorry.

I firmly intend, with your help,
to do penance,
to sin no more,
and to avoid whatever leads me to sin.

We promise not to sin again. We try to make up for our sins.

Our Savior Jesus Christ
suffered and died for us.
In his name, my God, have mercy.

We ask God to forgive us in Jesus' name.

Forgiveness and Peace

Explain to someone what happens in the sacrament of Reconciliation.

Is there someone to whom you need to say "I'm sorry?" Will you? How? Is there someone you need to forgive? Will you? How?

Listen to this song, then sing it. It tells about God's forgiveness. (To the tune of "Joyful, Joyful!")

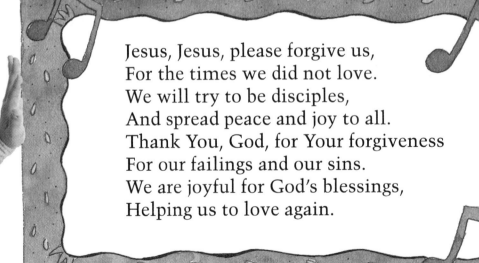

Jesus, Jesus, please forgive us,
For the times we did not love.
We will try to be disciples,
And spread peace and joy to all.
Thank You, God, for Your forgiveness
For our failings and our sins.
We are joyful for God's blessings,
Helping us to love again.

Pray the Act of Contrition. Then sing the song together.

Family Focus

You may want to begin going over this lesson by talking together about a recent incident in which a family member said "I'm sorry." Briefly discuss why it was important to say these words. Ask what your child thinks these words mean.

1. Then read through the opening stories together to see how well your child understands that being sorry for a sin may require more than words. We must make up with the person who has been hurt. We must promise not to sin again.

2. Invite your child to tell you the story of the woman Jesus forgave. Ask your child *why* Jesus forgave her. How did she say "I'm sorry"? Help your child sing the song about God's forgiveness and blessings.

3. In the sacrament of Reconciliation, we pray a special prayer of sorrow called an Act of Contrition. Help your child learn this prayer by heart. There are several acts of contrition that can be said. We are suggesting your child learn this one by heart.

4. Help your child with the **At Home** activity.

At Home

When we have done something wrong, we say:
"Please _____ me."
When a person has hurt us, we say:
"I _____ you." We have learned that when we are sorry, God will always _____ us.

Find the word by coloring only the "x" spaces.

Pray the Our Father together with your family.
Listen carefully for this word as you pray.

4 Examination of Conscience

Sit in a circle. As everyone sings the song, one child walks around the circle and taps someone on the shoulder. That person stands up and joins hands with the child outside the circle. The second child taps another who then joins the outside circle.

Sing the song (to the tune of "Go Round and Round the Village") until everyone is standing up holding hands.

♪ Go round and round God's love ring,
Go round and round God's love ring,
Go round and round God's love ring,
And find someone who cares. ♫

Talk about what it means to belong to God's love ring.
How do you know when you are living God's love?

Sometimes it is easy to tell right from wrong.
Sometimes it is hard to know the best
choices we should make.
What do you do to make good choices?
What questions do you ask?
What people help you?

Make up a prayer asking the Holy Spirit to
guide you. Share your prayer with a friend.

Jesus wanted us to know how much God
loves and cares for us — even when we do
things that are wrong. Here is a story He told.

The Lost Sheep

Once there was a shepherd who had one hundred sheep. He cared for all of them. One day one of the sheep got lost. The shepherd was so worried about the lost sheep that he left all the others to go and look for it.

After a long search, the shepherd found the lost sheep. He picked it up gently and carried it home on his shoulders.

The shepherd was full of joy. He called to his friends, "Come, and celebrate! I have found my lost sheep."

Then Jesus told the people that there is great joy in heaven when a sinner is truly sorry.
Based on Luke 15:4–7

Jesus is our Good Shepherd. He loves and cares for us. When we do what is wrong and are truly sorry, He is full of joy.

We Know Right from Wrong

In the story Jesus told, the lost sheep did not know it was doing something wrong.

People are different from sheep. We can know whether our choices are good or bad. We call this way of knowing right from wrong our conscience. Conscience helps us to know what is right and what is wrong.

Before we celebrate the sacrament of Reconciliation, we ask God the Holy Spirit to help us remember our sins. This is called an examination of conscience.

We think about the times we made a bad choice, or did what was wrong. We also remember the times we should have done good things but did not. We ask ourselves whether we have been living as Jesus wants us to live.

Here are some questions to help you to examine your conscience.

An Examination of Conscience

1. When I make choices, do I sometimes forget to think first about what God wants me to do? Have I done what God wants?

2. Have I used the name of God or Jesus in a bad way?

3. Did I worship God at Mass each Sunday?

4. Have I disobeyed the grown-ups who take care of me?

5. Have I been angry with or cruel to others?

6. Have I forgotten to show respect for my body and the bodies of others?

7. Have I taken anything that is not mine or treated others unfairly?

8. Have I always told the truth?

9. Have I hurt someone by what I have said or done? Have I been jealous of others?

10. Have I refused to help people who are in need? Have I been selfish?

The Good Shepherd

Act out the story of the lost sheep with your friends. Show how you think the sheep felt when it was lost, and how it felt to be found. How did the shepherd feel when he found and carried his sheep home?

Now be very still. Listen to the music. Then sing the song as a prayer to end your lesson.

Always Ready to Forgive
Carey Landry

♪ You are always ready to forgive, O Lord, always ready to forgive. When we come to you with sorrow in our hearts, you are always ready to forgive.

Like a shepherd searching for a lamb that has strayed, looking and searching ev'rywhere. When he finds that lamb he takes her in his arms; he embraces her and carries her home. ♪

Family Focus

This lesson on examination of conscience is a very important one for young children. It should be presented in the context of the love and care God has for them especially as expressed, at least in part, in the love and care they experience at home and in the faith community. We do not want our children to become guilt-ridden or scrupulous. Yet we must help them become aware of their responsibilities as baptized members of the Church. We also want to help them to become aware of the great love and mercy of Christ, who supports them when they do what is right and who forgives them when they do what is wrong.

Conscience is that awareness we have about the rightness or wrongness of our choices. In young children it should be developed gently and consistently.

1. Read through the lesson together. Invite your child to tell you the story of the lost sheep. Ask how we are like the lost sheep when we do what is wrong.

2. Go over the questions for an examination of conscience on page 35. Your child might want to suggest other or different questions. You might want to add ones that you find helpful.

3. Pray together the words of the song your child learned on page 36. Then help your child do the **At Home** activity.

At Home

Help the shepherd find the lost sheep. Use a crayon or marker.

After you help the shepherd find the lost sheep, pray this prayer with your family.

† Jesus, You are our Good Shepherd. You guide and protect us. Help us always to make loving choices. Amen.

5 Celebrating Reconciliation

Act out this gospel play together.

Reader 1: A man named Zacchaeus lived in the town of Jericho. He was a tax collector and a very rich man. The people of the town did not like him because he had cheated them.

One day Jesus was going to Jericho. A large crowd had gathered to see Him. Zacchaeus also wanted to see Jesus. But Zacchaeus could not see over the people's heads because he was short.

Zacchaeus: I can't see Jesus! I know what I'll do. I'll climb up this tree.

Reader 2: So Zacchaeus climbed the tree. Soon Jesus came by. He looked up and said,

Jesus: Zacchaeus, come down quickly! I want to stay at your house today.

Reader 3: Zacchaeus jumped down. He was so happy! Jesus wanted to stay at *his* house.

All: (grumbling) Jesus is going to stay at the house of this tax collector. Zacchaeus is a sinner. He cheated us.

Zacchaeus: Jesus, I am sorry I have done wrong things. I am going to give half of all I have to the poor. If I have cheated anyone, I promise to give back four times what I owe.

Reader 4: Jesus knew Zacchaeus was truly sorry for his sins. Jesus forgave Zacchaeus. He said,

Jesus: Today, Zacchaeus, I bring you forgiveness and peace.

All: (To the tune of "Did You Ever See a Lassie?")
♫ Oh, we are friends of Jesus, our Brother and Shepherd.
Jesus teaches us to love and to follow His way.
Our friends and our family will help us get ready.
For Your peace and Your forgiveness, dear Jesus, we pray. ♫

Why do you think Jesus forgave Zacchaeus?
Why do you think Jesus forgives us?

The Sacrament of Peace

Jesus shares with us God's forgiveness and peace in a special way in the sacrament of Reconciliation. He forgives our sins. Jesus makes us one again with Him and with the Church.

Jesus gave His apostles the power to forgive sins in His name. Jesus said to them, "Receive the Holy Spirit. Whose sins you shall forgive will be forgiven." By the power of the Holy Spirit, the priest forgives sins in Jesus' name, too.

We can celebrate the sacrament of Reconciliation in two ways. We can celebrate the sacrament *alone* with the priest. Or we can also celebrate the sacrament *together* with the priest and our parish family.

In each of these celebrations, we go one by one to talk to the priest. We can talk to him face-to-face or from behind a screen. We tell our sins to God by telling them to the priest. This is called making our *confession*.

In both ways of celebrating Reconciliation, we tell God we are sorry for our sins. We promise not to sin again. God forgives us, and we are at peace with God and one another.

Individual Rite of Reconciliation

When we celebrate Reconciliation by ourselves with the priest, this is what we do.

- We get ready to celebrate the sacrament by making an examination of conscience.

- We go into the reconciliation room to meet with the priest. He greets us in God's name and in the name of the Church. We make the sign of the cross together.

- We listen. The priest may read a story to us from the Bible about God's love and forgiveness.

- We confess our sins to God. We do this by telling our sins to the priest. The priest will never tell anyone what we say in confession!

- The priest helps us remember how Jesus wants us to love God and one another. We promise not to sin again. The priest then gives us a penance. A *penance* is a prayer or good work we do to show God we are sorry.

- We pray an act of contrition. We promise to try not to sin again.

- The priest prays the words of absolution. *Absolution* means that our sins are forgiven.

- We thank God because our sins have been forgiven in this wonderful sacrament. We know that we are God's friends. We are at peace.

43

Celebrating with Others

When we celebrate the sacrament of Reconciliation with the priest and with other people in our parish, here is what we do.

* We gather with our parish family and sing a song. The priest welcomes us in the name of the whole Church.

* We listen to a story from the Bible about God's mercy. The priest or deacon explains the story. He reminds us that God always loves us and that God forgives us when we are sorry for our sins.

* We examine our conscience. We think about the times we may not have lived as followers of Jesus.

* Together we pray an act of contrition and the Our Father. We ask God to help us not to sin again.

* The priest meets with us one by one. We make our confession. Remember, the priest never tells anyone what we say to him!

* The priest gives us a penance.

* Then the priest says the words of absolution. This means that our sins are forgiven.

* After all have had a turn to meet with the priest alone for confession, we gather together again.

- We thank God because our sins have been forgiven. We are sure that we are God's friends.
- The priest blesses us. He asks us to bring Jesus' peace to others.
- We sing a song to thank God for forgiving us.

Celebrating Reconciliation

These steps are always part of the celebration of the sacrament of Reconciliation.

- We examine our conscience and are sorry for our sins. We promise not to sin again.
- We confess our sins to the priest.
- We receive a penance.
- We pray an act of contrition.
- The priest gives us absolution, and we thank God for His mercy.

We Prepare

With your group, visit the reconciliation room in your parish church. Talk about the things you see there. Choose the way you would like to receive the sacrament.

Share together your thoughts and feelings about celebrating the sacrament of Reconciliation for the first time.

What else will you do to prepare to celebrate this wonderful sacrament of God's peace?

Cut out the heart in the back of the book. Pray the prayer. Attach a ribbon to the heart and place it around your neck. Then sing *My First Reconciliation Song* together.

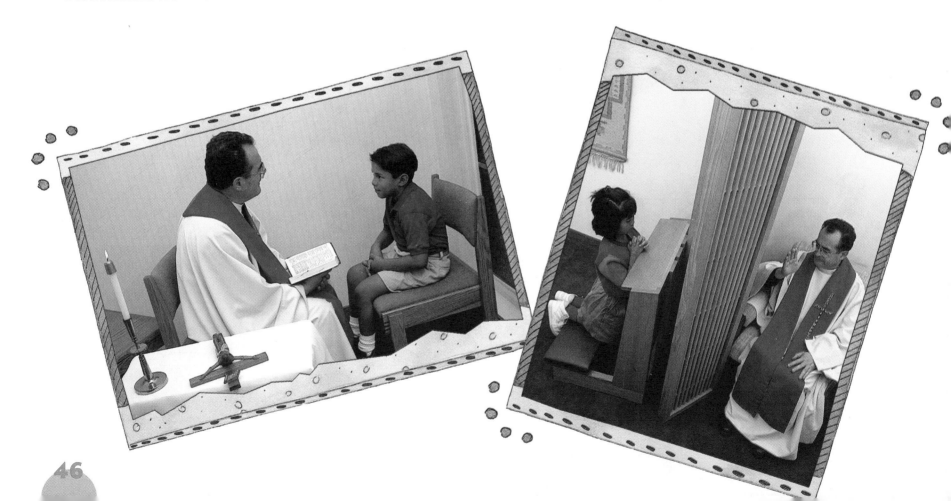

In this lesson your child has been introduced to two ways we celebrate the sacrament of Reconciliation: by ourselves with the priest and together with the priest and the community.

Your child may be a little confused or nervous about what will happen at First Reconciliation. Go over the lesson slowly and confidently. This will help your child to look forward to this new milestone.

1. Invite family members to take part in the opening gospel play. Then read through the lesson together. Help your child come to a beginning understanding of the *communal* effects of sin. Because we are united to one another in Christ, the loving or unloving choices we make affect the whole community.

2. Gently take your child through the steps of the celebration. Encourage your child to choose the way he or she is most comfortable in celebrating the sacrament. Review the Act of Contrition with your child. See page 27.

3. Summarize by going over the five simple steps on page 45.

4. Invite the whole family to take part in the **At Home** activity.

At Home

The choices we make affect everyone around us, especially the members of our families. Our loving choices help us to grow. Make a "Loving Choices Tree" like the one below for your family.

Draw a branch for each family member. When someone makes a loving choice, add a leaf to that person's branch.

6 Living as Peacemakers

Gather in a circle. Be very still as you look at the picture. Imagine that you are one of the children in this Bible story.

Let Them Come to Me

One day some mothers and fathers brought their children to Jesus. They wanted Jesus to lay His hands on the children and bless them.

Jesus had been teaching the people all day. There was a crowd all around Him. The disciples saw the children and their parents trying to reach Jesus. They stopped them.

"Take the children away," the disciples said. "Jesus is too busy."

Jesus said, "No, do not send them away." He called the children to Him. He put His hands on their heads and blessed them. Jesus loved children very much. He said to His disciples,

"Let the children come to Me and do not stop them. The kingdom of God belongs to children like these."

Based on Mark 10:13–16

Imagine you are one of the children close to Jesus. What do you say to Him?
What does He say to you?
How do you feel? What will you do?

After Reconciliation

Parish Pancake Breakfast

We should try to celebrate the sacrament of Reconciliation often. We celebrate it especially to prepare for important times in the Church year such as Christmas and Easter.

When we celebrate the sacrament of Reconciliation, we are like the children with Jesus. He doesn't want anything to keep us from being with Him. He wants us to be filled with His peace. We are friends with Jesus. We are at peace with ourselves and with all God's people.

Jesus wants us to share His peace with our families, with our parish community, and with everyone we meet.

How to Bring Peace to Others

We can:

- live the Law of Love and the Ten Commandments.
- be thankful for God's forgiveness and forgive others.
- be kind and loving members of the Church both at home and at school.
- try to help those who are not being treated justly or kindly.

How can you bring the peace of Jesus to someone today?

Saint Francis of Assisi was a great peacemaker. His special prayer will remind you of ways you can share the peace of Jesus with others. Join together to pray his prayer.

Prayer of Saint Francis

Lord, make me an instrument of Your peace:
where there is hatred, let me sow love;
where there is injury, pardon;
where there is doubt, faith;
where there is despair, hope;
where there is darkness, light;
where there is sadness, joy.

Congratulations! You have been a good shepherd to your First Reconciliation child. In preparing your child for this healing sacrament, you have been a minister of reconciliation and peace. Continue to encourage your child, in word and example, to have a positive attitude toward this sacrament of God's mercy. It is most important to help your child to become comfortable with the sacrament by celebrating it often.

This closing lesson is a very important part of your child's understanding that the sacrament lives on in us as we go forth to obey the Law of Love, to honor the Ten Commandments, to act justly, and to make peace with others.

Begin this session by embracing your child and thanking him or her for being so faithful in preparing for First Reconciliation.

1. Invite your child to tell you the story of Jesus and the children. Share the follow-up questions.

2. Talk about what we do as Jesus' peacemakers after we celebrate the sacrament. Then pray together the prayer of Saint Francis on page 52.

3. Help your child to do the **At Home** activity.

At Home

How can you share the peace of Christ with others?

Make a circle of peace to hang near your front door. On one side print the words "Christ's Peace to All." On the other side find pictures that show peace. You can use family photos that show peaceful times.

1. Cut out two circles of the same size.
2. After decorating the circles glue them back-to-back.
3. Punch a hole at the top. Put a string through to use as a hanger.

A Peacemaking Rite

Child 1: Our parish family is rejoicing with us. We have celebrated the sacrament of Reconciliation for the first time. Jesus has given us His healing gift of peace. Jesus said, "Peace I leave you, My peace I give to you." Let us share with one another a sign of God's peace.

Now let us join together in prayer and thanksgiving.

Child 2: For the gift of God's peace given to us in the sacrament of Reconciliation,

All: Jesus, we thank You.

Child 3: For the help of our family and friends,

All: Jesus, we thank You.

Child 4: For teaching us to share love and peace with others,

All: Jesus, we thank You.

Leader: Parents, you have prepared your children to celebrate this wonderful sacrament of mercy and forgiveness.

When your child's name is called, please come forward with your child to receive the certificate.

Now let us join hands and pray the prayer that helps us to be peacemakers: Our Father. . . .

Let There Be Peace on Earth
Sy Miller and Jill Jackson

♪ Let there be peace on earth
And let it begin with me.
Let there be peace on earth
A peace that was meant to be.

With God as our Father
We are family.
Let us walk now together
In perfect harmony.

Let peace begin with me;
Let this be the moment now.
With every step I take
Let this be my solemn vow:
To take each moment and
Live each moment
In peace eternally.
Let there be peace on earth
And let it begin with me! ♪

Summary: I Will Remember

1. What is the Law of Love?

The Law of Love is "You must love God with all your heart. You must love others as you love yourself."

2. What are the Ten Commandments?

The Ten Commandments are laws that tell us what God wants us to do. They help us to live healthy and happy lives.

3. What is sin?

Sin is freely choosing to do what we know to be wrong. It means disobeying God's law on purpose.

4. What is the sacrament of Reconciliation?

Reconciliation is the sacrament in which we celebrate God's mercy and forgiveness of our sins.

5. What steps are always part of the sacrament of Reconciliation?

We examine our conscience; we confess our sins; we receive a penance; we pray an act of contrition; we receive absolution.

6. What do we do after Reconciliation?

After Reconciliation, we share the peace of Jesus with our families, our parish community, and with everyone we meet.

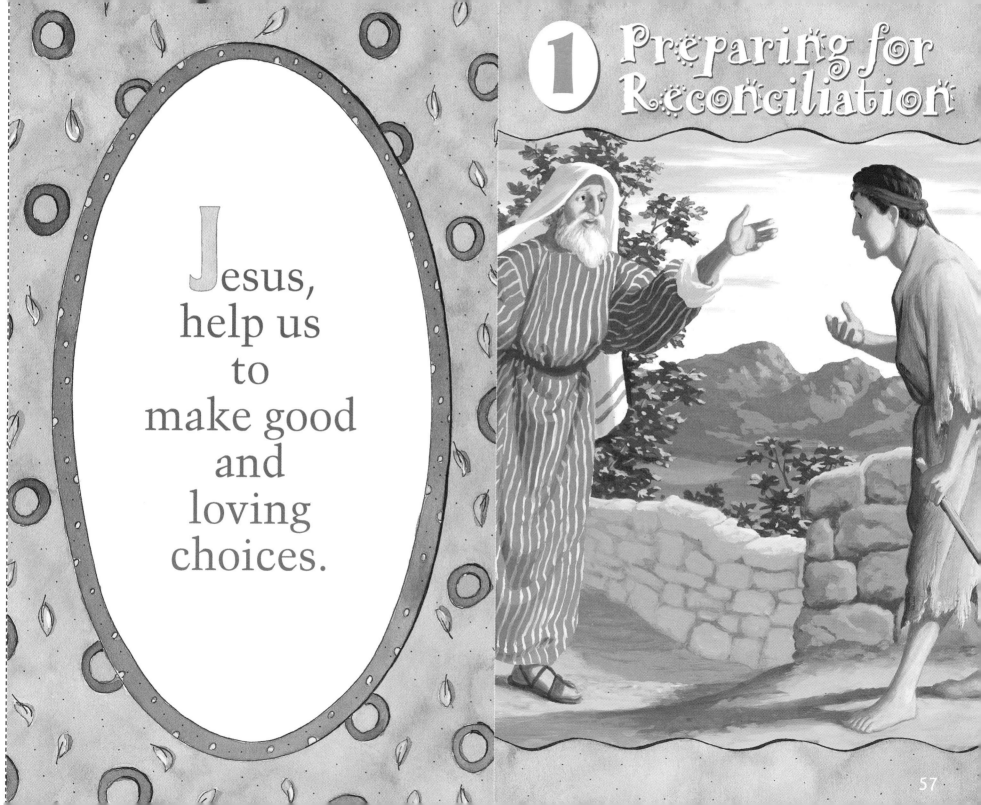

Jesus,
help us
to
make good
and
loving
choices.

I am preparing to celebrate Reconciliation

1. Jesus helps us to make good and loving

   _____.

2. To make a right choice, we begin by asking

   the _____ _____ to help us.

3. Mistakes and accidents are not

   _____.

I remember God's word

Show how the son found his way home. Color the stones as you choose the correct words to fill in the story.

A loving father had _____ sons.

One son made a _____ choice and left home.

Then he was _____ and came home again.

He made a _____ choice.

His father said, "Let's celebrate!

My son was lost and now he is _____!"

FOLD

Loving
God,
You always
forgive us
when
we
are sorry.

I am preparing to celebrate Reconciliation

1. When we love God, others, and ourselves we

   are living the _____ of

   _____.

2. Freely choosing to do what we know is

   wrong is _____.

3. The _____ _____

   tell us what God wants us to do to show

   our love.

I remember God's word

Jesus said the greatest commandment is:
Love the Lord your God with all your heart,
  8   6   2

with all your soul, and with all your mind.
                     4   3

Love your neighbor as you love yourself.
1   9   7   5

What do we call this greatest commandment?
Use the numbered letters above to find the
answer.

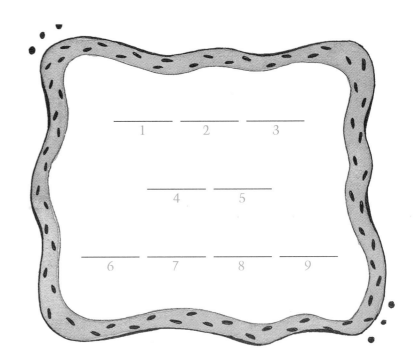

___ ___ ___
 1   2   3

___ ___
 4   5

___ ___ ___ ___
 6   7   8   9

FOLD

Thank You,
Jesus,
for joy,
forgiveness,
and
peace!

I am preparing to celebrate Reconciliation

1. Jesus forgives us, no matter what we have

   done, when we are _____.

2. Being sorry means making up, or being

   _____, with those we have hurt.

3. A special prayer of sorrow is called the

   _____ of _____.

I remember God's word

Finish the Bible story. Write the words in the puzzle.

One day Jesus was invited to Simon's house for dinner. A woman who was a sinner came in.

1. She was _____ for her sins.

2. Jesus forgave her because of her great _____.

3. He said, "Your sins are _____.

4. Go in _____."

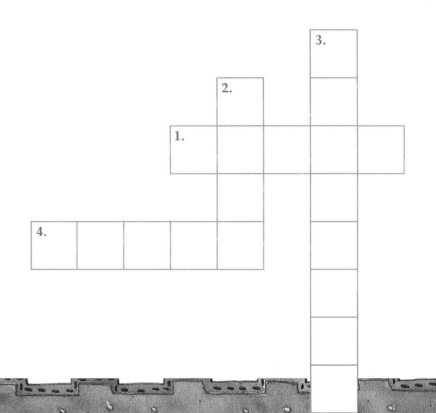

Jesus,
our
Good Shepherd,
You find us
if we are lost.
You gently
lead us
back home.
Jesus,
Your love
and care
never ends.

I am preparing to celebrate Reconciliation

1. Our _____ tells us when we are not loving God or others.

2. We ask the _____ _____ to help us think about the choices we make.

3. When we ask ourselves whether we have been living as Jesus wants we _____ our _____.

FOLD

I remember God's word

Tell why Jesus is like the shepherd in the story of the lost sheep.

_____

_____

_____

_____

_____

_____

_____

_____

Jesus,
bless my
heart
to
know
Your love!

I am preparing to celebrate Reconciliation

1. Jesus gave His disciples the power to

   _____ _____ in

   His name.

2. Telling our sins to God by telling them to

   the priest is making our _____.

3. A prayer or good work to show we are sorry

   is a _____.

I remember God's word

Unscramble the letters to complete each sentence. Then read the Bible story.

Zacchaeus wanted to see _____.

sesJu

Zacchaeus was so _____ he climbed a tree.

rhsto

Jesus stopped and talked to _____.

hcaZcsuea

Zacchaeus felt _____ for cheating people.

yrosr

Zacchaeus _____ to give back

mpdoesri
anything he had taken.

Jesus _____ Zacchaeus because he

gefrova
was truly sorry.

What does Jesus want us to do when we have done something wrong?

FOLD

6 Preparing for Reconciliation

Lord,
make me
an
instrument
of
Your
peace!

I am preparing to celebrate Reconciliation

1. Jesus wants us to share His _____ with everyone.

2. We bring peace to others when we live God's _____ of _____.

3. When we need forgiveness we should celebrate the sacrament of _____.

I remember God's word

Complete each sentence. Then find and circle your answers in the letter box.

One day some mothers and fathers

brought their _____ to Jesus.

They wanted Jesus to _____ their children.

The disciples said, "Take the children _____.

Jesus is too _____."

Jesus said, "No! Let the children _____

to _____."

```
C  X  O  C  J  L  P  T
O  R  U  H  M  Q  M  E
M  S  A  I  S  B  C  D
E  N  B  L  E  S  S  S
P  B  Q  D  O  U  I  E
Z  U  Y  R  A  W  A  Y
O  S  A  E  R  T  W  N
A  Y  C  N  K  J  D  S
```

FOLD

Celebrating Reconciliation with Others

We sing an opening hymn and the priest greets us.
The priest prays an opening prayer.

We listen to a reading from the Bible and a homily.

We examine our conscience.
We make an act of contrition.

We may say a prayer or sing a song,
and then pray the Our Father.

We confess our sins to the priest. In the name
of God and the Christian community, the priest
gives us a penance and absolution.

We pray as we conclude our celebration.
The priest blesses us, and we go in
the peace and joy of Christ.

Celebrating Reconciliation by Myself

The priest greets me.

I make the sign of the cross.
The priest asks me to trust in God's mercy.

He or I may read a story from the Bible.

I talk with the priest about myself.
I confess my sins: what I did wrong and why.
The priest talks to me about loving God and others.
He gives me a penance.

I make an act of contrition.
In the name of God and the Church,
the priest gives me absolution. (He may extend or
place his hands on my head.)
This means that God has forgiven my sins.

Together, the priest and I give thanks
for God's forgiveness.

Prayers

Our Father

Our Father, who art in heaven,
hallowed be thy name;
thy kingdom come;
thy will be done on earth
as it is in heaven.
Give us this day our daily bread;
and forgive us our trespasses
as we forgive those
who trespass against us;
and lead us not into temptation,
but deliver us from evil.
Amen.

Hail Mary

Hail Mary, full of grace,
the Lord is with you;
blessed are you among women,
and blessed is the fruit of your
womb, Jesus.
Holy Mary, Mother of God,
pray for us sinners now
and at the hour of our death.
Amen.

Glory to the Father

Glory to the Father,
and to the Son,
and to the Holy Spirit:
as it was in the beginning,
is now, and will be for ever.
Amen.

Morning Offering

My God, I offer You today
all I think and do and say,
uniting it with what was done
on earth by Jesus Christ,
Your Son.

Evening Prayer

Dear God, before I sleep I want
to thank You for this day so
full of Your kindness and Your joy.
I close my eyes to rest safe
in Your loving care.

Prayers

Prayer of Quiet

Sit in a comfortable position.
Relax by breathing in and out.
Shut out all sights and sounds.
Each time you breathe in and
out, say the name "Jesus."

Psalm of Praise

O God,
Your greatness is seen in all
   the world.

Based on Psalm 8:9

Psalm of Sorrow

Remember, God, Your
   kindness and constant love.
Forgive my sins.

Based on Psalm 25:6–7

Psalm of Thanksgiving

I thank You, God, with all
   my heart.
I sing praises to You.

Based on Psalm 138:1

Psalm of Trust

May Your constant love
   be with us, O God,
as we put our hope in You.

Based on Psalm 33:22

Psalm for Help

Remember me, O God, when
   You help Your people.

Based on Psalm 106:4

Act of Contrition

See page 27.

A Peacemaker Checklist

Here is a checklist to help you and your family keep on the "right track" to peace. Each time you follow the road to peace, draw a happy face in the circle. Together help one another to live as God's peacemakers.

I celebrated God's forgiveness in the sacrament of Reconciliation.

I showed I was sorry for an unloving choice.

I _____

I helped to make someone feel better.

Peace and Happiness

I said "I am sorry" when I made an unloving choice.

I told the truth.

I said "I forgive you" when someone was sorry for hurting me.

I shared what I had with someone.

We, the _____ Family, are God's peacemakers!

Being God's Peacemakers

Think of another way that you live as
God's peacemakers.

Write it in the space on the track.

Now carefully cut on the broken line.
Hang your peacemaker checklist in a special place.

Make time during the week
to go over the checklist
with your family.

Prayer Partners

A prayer partner can be anyone—old or young, boy or girl, near or far away. This person is special. As you prepare to receive God's gift of forgiveness in Reconciliation, your prayer partner helps you. He or she remembers you in thought and prayer.

Ask your teacher for the name of a home-bound person or a person in a nursing home. You can also help this person. By asking him or her to become your prayer partner, you will help this person feel needed and special.

Complete the letter on this page. Remember to put your name. You can add your own special message, too. Then carefully cut on the broken lines to send your message.

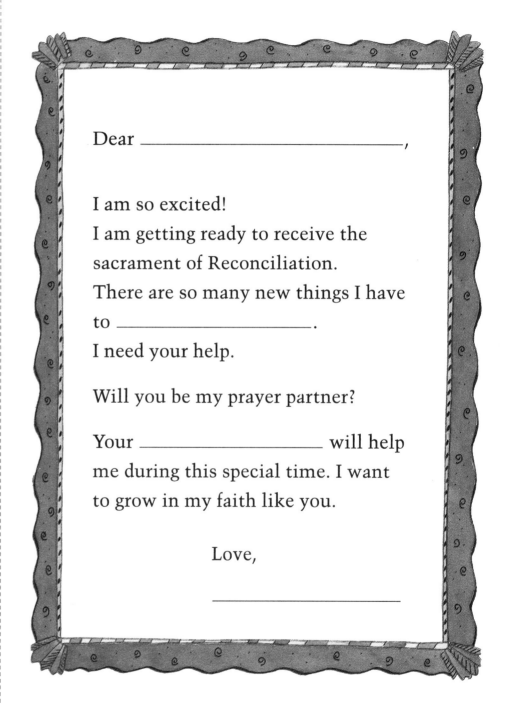

Dear _____,

I am so excited!
I am getting ready to receive the
sacrament of Reconciliation.
There are so many new things I have
to _____.
I need your help.

Will you be my prayer partner?

Your _____ will help
me during this special time. I want
to grow in my faith like you.

Love,

_____

An Invitation

An Invitation

You are being asked to
support this young person with
your "prayer and care"
during these weeks of preparation
for the sacrament of Reconciliation.
We hope that
you will join with us
at this special time.

(FOLD)

More Songs for Reconciliation

God Has Made Us a Family

Carey Landry

(can be used with Chapter 2)

God has made us a family and together
we will grow in love.
God has made us a family and together
we will grow in love.

1. Oh, Yes! We need one another,
   as together we grow in love;
   and we will forgive one another,
   as together we grow in love.

2. We will reach out to those in need,
   as we learn to grow in love;
   to those who are lonely and hurting,
   as we learn to grow in love.

We Come to Ask Forgiveness

Carey Landry

(can be used with Chapter 3)

We come to ask your forgiveness, O Lord,
and we seek forgiveness from each other.
Sometimes we build up walls instead of
bridges to peace,
and we ask your forgiveness, O Lord.

1. Sometimes we hurt by what we do to
   others. Sometimes we hurt with words
   that are untrue. Sometimes we cause
   others pain by what we fail to do and we
   ask your forgiveness, O Lord.

2. For the time when we've been rude and
   selfish; for the times when we have been
   unkind; and for the times we refused to
   help our friends in need, we ask your
   forgiveness, O Lord.

More Songs for Reconciliation

New Hope

Carey Landry

(can be used with Chapter 5)

1. New hope, new hope is what we have
   been given by the Lord;
   new hope, new hope is what we have
   been given by the Lord.★★

★★Alleluia, Alleluia, Alleluia, Lord;
Alleluia, Alleluia, Alleluia, Lord.

2. New life, new life is what we have
   been given by the Lord;
   new life, new life is what we have
   been given by the Lord.★★

3. A new heart, a new heart is what we have
   been given by the Lord;
   A new heart, a new heart is what we have
   been given by the Lord.★★

Peace to You and Me

Carey Landry

(can be used with Chapter 6)

Peace to you; peace to me;
peace to each of us.
From me to you and you to me,
we bring the gift of peace.

1. The peace that we live;
   the peace that we give is
   the peace of Christ.
   In giving forgiveness,
   love and care, we share the
   gift of peace.

2. From one to one, then
   on and on, we share the
   gift of peace. From all who
   give to all who receive,
   we share the gift of peace.

Certificate
of
First Reconciliation

The parish of

_____

embraces with the merciful love of God

_____

who celebrated for the first time
the
Sacrament of Reconciliation

on _____ in _____

Pastor _____